FOUL DEEDS & SUSPICIOUS DEATHS IN LONDON'S WEST END

FOUL DEEDS AND SUSPICIOUS DEATHS Series

Wharncliffe's *Foul Deeds and Suspicious Deaths* series explores, in detail, crimes of passion, brutal murders and foul misdemeanours from early modern times to the present day. Victorian street crime, mysterious death and modern murders tell tales where passion, jealousy and social deprivation brought unexpected violence to those involved. From unexplained death and suicide to murder and manslaughter, the books provide a fascinating insight into the lives of both victims and perpetrators as well as society as a whole.

Other titles in the series include:

Foul Deeds and Suspicious Deaths in Birmingham, Nick Billingham
ISBN: 1-903425-96-4. £10.99

Foul Deeds and Suspicious Deaths in Bolton, Glynis Cooper
ISBN: 1-903425-63-8. £9.99

Foul Deeds and Suspicious Deaths in Colchester, Patrick Denney
ISBN: 1-903425-80-8. £10.99

Foul Deeds and Suspicious Deaths in Coventry, David McGrory
ISBN: 1-903425-57-3. £ 9.99

Foul Deeds and Suspicious Deaths Around Derby, Kevin Turton
ISBN: 1-903425-76-x. £9.99

Foul Deeds and Suspicious Deaths in & around Durham, Maureen Anderson
ISBN: 1-903425-46-8. £9.99

Foul Deeds and Suspicious Deaths in London's East End, Geoffrey Howse
ISBN: 1-903425-71-9. £10.99

Foul Deeds and Suspicious Deaths in Hampstead, Holburn & St Pancras, Mark Aston
ISBN: 1-903425-94-8. £10.99

Foul Deeds and Suspicious Deaths in Hull, David Goodman
ISBN: 1-903425-43-3. £9.99

Foul Deeds and Suspicious Deaths Around Leicester, Kevin Turton
ISBN: 1-903425-75-1. £10.99

Foul Deeds and Suspicious Deaths in Manchester, Martin Baggoley
ISBN: 1-903425-65-4. £9.99

Foul Deeds and Suspicious Deaths in Newcastle, Maureen Anderson
ISBN: 1-903425-34-4. £9.99

Foul Deeds and Suspicious Deaths in Newport, Terry Underwood
ISBN: 1-903425-59-X. £9.99

Foul Deeds and Suspicious Deaths in and Around Scunthorpe, Stephen Wade
ISBN: 1-903425-88-3. £9.99

More Foul Deeds and Suspicious Deaths in Wakefield, Kate Taylor
ISBN: 1-903425-48-4. £9.99

Foul Deeds and Suspicious Deaths in York, Keith Henson
ISBN: 1-903425-33-6. £9.99

Foul Deeds and Suspicious Deaths on the Yorkshire Coast, Alan Whitworth
ISBN: 1-903425-01-8. £9.99

Please contact us via any of the methods below for more information or a catalogue.
WHARNCLIFFE BOOKS
47 Church Street – Barnsley – South Yorkshire – S70 2AS
Tel: 01226 734555 – 734222 Fax: 01226 734438
E-mail: enquiries@pen-and-sword.co.uk – Website: www.wharncliffebooks.co.uk

Foul Deeds & Suspicious Deaths in
LONDON'S WEST END

GEOFFREY HOWSE

Series Editor
Brian Elliott

Wharncliffe Books

Dedication

*This book is dedicated to a
true Londoner*

Tracy P Deller
Who loves the West End

**First Published in Great Britain in 2006 by
Wharncliffe Books**
an imprint of
**Pen and Sword Books Ltd
47 Church Street
Barnsley
South Yorkshire
S70 2AS**

Copyright © Geoffrey Howse 2006

ISBN: Paperback 1-84563-001-7

Typeset in 11/13pt Plantin by Mac Style, Nafferton, E. Yorkshire

Printed and bound in England by
CPI UK.

Pen and Sword Books Ltd incorporates the Imprints of
Pen & Sword Aviation, Pen & Sword Maritime,
Pen & Sword Military, Wharncliffe Books,
Pen & Sword Select, Pen and Sword Military Classics
and Leo Cooper.

For a complete list of Pen & Sword titles please contact
PEN & SWORD BOOKS LIMITED
47 Church Street
Barnsley
South Yorkshire
S70 2BR
England
E-mail: enquiries@pen-and-sword.co.uk
Website: www.pen-and-sword.co.uk

Contents

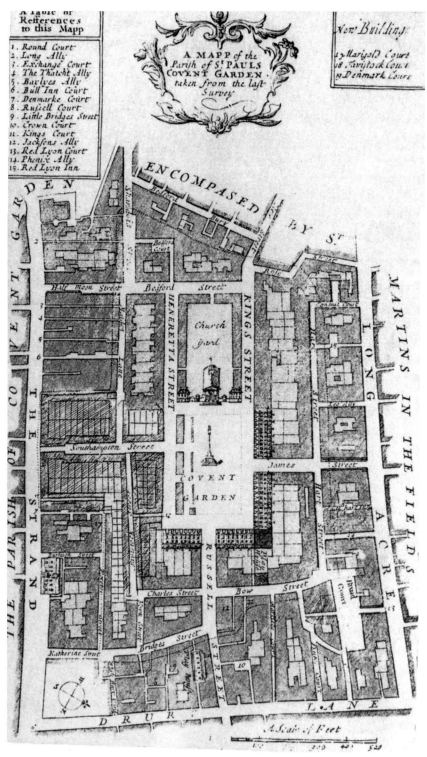

A Map of the Parish of St Paul's, Covent Garden from Stow's Survey of 1755. Author's collection

Introduction

London's West End, as distinct from West London, which is quite different in all respects (West London being those relatively modern London Boroughs to the West of the metropolis, the West End being at the heart of it), is contained within a relatively small area. The West End is not as clearly defined as that part of London popularly referred to as the 'Square Mile', the City of London, which has remained London's financial district since the ancient Roman city was founded over two thousand years ago. The West End is largely situated within the 'other city', the City of Westminster, founded a thousand years later. The City of Westminster grew around Westminster Abbey, founded by Edward the Confessor, Saint and English King, born *c.*1003, who reigned from 1042–66, and his palace of Westminster, now the Houses of Parliament. The West End of today lies largely within Westminster itself, and partly in the modern London Borough of Camden and the Royal Borough of Kensington and Chelsea. As well as incorporating some of the most famous theatres, hotels, shopping streets and arcades in the world, the West End has been, for centuries, the place where the monarch and other members of the Royal Family, aristocratic, noble, wealthy, fashionable and famous, usually kept a London residence. The West End's identity has always been jealously guarded to keep it special and to distinguish it from that part of London east of the Tower of London known as the East End, which has a very distinctive character and history, but not as those from the West End would have it, as important and distinguished as their own. Whereas the East End largely grew up along the River Thames and the eleven Tower Hamlets, over many centuries, dating principally from early Norman times, the West End's development as a fashionable area of any significance can be roughly dated to the closing decades of the sixteenth century, when the area began to be developed on a large scale and theatres and other places of entertainment became an important feature. Despite the supposed gentility of the West End, there has been a considerable amount of foul deeds perpetrated there, as you will see in the chapters that follow.

The West End consists of parts of the City of Westminster and includes Mayfair, Belgravia, parts of Victoria, Knightsbridge, Bayswater, Marylebone, Fitzrovia, Holborn and Bloomsbury, Strand, Piccadilly, St James's, Adelphi, St Giles, St Martin's, Soho and Covent Garden. Within these areas are other smaller districts which have their own individual characters. The present day Oxford Street, formerly known as Tyburn Road, could be said to bisect the West End but not quite in equal portions. It was along this thoroughfare that condemned prisoners were brought on their way to be executed at Tyburn, situated where Edgeware Road meets Oxford Street in the vicinity of Marble Arch.

Within the pages of this book you will find many references to Tyburn and to prisoners being drawn to their executions there. To clarify what *drawing* actually meant and to avoid confusion, here is a brief explanation. There were three kinds of drawing. In the vast majority of cases drawing means dragging to the place of execution, where hanging disemboweling and quartering followed. But drawing sometimes means dragging till the sufferer died of the mere dragging. In some cases drawing means tugging by horses in opposite directions till the sufferer was torn to pieces. Drawing in any of its forms appears to have been extremely unpleasant, and usually had only one outcome, death.

I have attempted to present as truthful and honest account as possible and wherever practicable have given my source information. I apologize unreservedly for any errors or omissions.

An early nineteenth century engraving of an execution outside Newgate Gaol. Author's collection

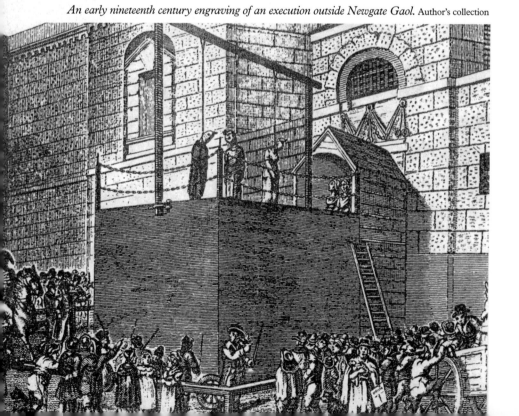

Acknowledgements

Iris Ackroyd, Keith Atack, Vera Atack, Susan Barnes, Anna Blackburn, Joan Bostwick, Christine Boyce, Robert (Bob) Alan Dale, Kathleen Dale, Iris J Deller, Joanna C Murray Deller, Ricky S Deller, James Friend, John Goldfinch, Doris Hayes, Ann Howse, Doreen Howse, Kathleen Howse, Richard Huggett (1929–2000), Dr Hidayat Hussein, Tammy Jones, Brendan E McNally, John Marsh, Eleanor Nelder, Stanley Nelder, Dr Declan O'Reilly, Jackie Thomas, Julia Wiggett, Helen Vodden, Katie Vollens, Adam R Walker, Christine Walker, Darren J Walker, David Walker, Ivan P Walker, Paula L Walker, Suki B Walker, Dave Webster and Terry Webster of D Webster and son, Clifford Willoughby, Margaret Willoughby, Whittington Hospital social work team, the staff of the British Library, the staff of the British Library Newspaper Archive, Colindale, the staff of the Guildhall Library, the staff of the National Archive, Kew. I would particularly like to thank John D Murray who has assisted me over many years.

The Idle Apprentice executed at Tyburn, as depicted by William Hogarth (1697–1764)
Author's collection

CHAPTER 1

Foul Deeds and Murder through the Ages, 1236–1984

Tyburn Tree has its First Victims 1236

... he should hang so long as anything should be left whole of him.

I n *Tyburn Tree Its History And Annals* by Alfred Marks, a fascinating volume which refers to the text of many rare and ancient documents, what is believed to be the first record of Tyburn Tree reads:

1236 About this time some bold but rash nobles in England, seduced by we know not what spirit, conspired together, and entered into an execrable alliance to ravage England like robbers and night-thieves. Their design, however, became known, and the chief of the conspiracy – to wit, Peter de Buffer, one of the king's doorkeepers – was taken prisoner, and by him others were accused. In order to whose execution a dreadful machine called a gibbet, was set up in London, and on it two of the chief conspirators were hanged, after having engaged in single combat. One of them was killed in the fight, and was hanged with his

The site of Tyburn Tree on the traffic island at the junction of Edgeware Road with Bayswater and Oxford Street, close to Marble Arch. A bronze plaque, close to the bollard in the right foreground, marks the spot. The author

head cleft open, and the other, hanged alive, breathed forth and his wretched life on the same gibbet amid the lamentations of the assembled multitude.

Execution of a Spy 1295

… he should hang so long as anything should be left whole of him.

Having being discovered spying for the French and found guilty of treason, judgement on Sir Thomas Turberville was pronounced by Sir Robert Brabazun, on the great dais in Westminster Hall, that he should be:

… drawn and hanged, and that he should hang so long as anything should be left whole of him.

Sir Thomas was drawn on a fresh ox-hide, and one chronicler wrote that he was so drawn that he might not die too quickly. He was drawn from Westminster to the Conduit of London in Cheapside, and then back into the West End to the gallows at Tyburn.

Cruel Deaths of the Scottish Patriots 1305 & 1306

If he is of nobler blood than the other parricides, he shall be hanged higher than they.

On 23 August 1305, Sir William Wallace, champion of Scottish independence (captured near Glasgow and brought to London), was firstly drawn from Westminster to the Tower of London and from there to the place of execution, where he was hanged on a specially constructed high gallows, before being cut down alive, disembowelled and quartered. The place of execution as most chroniclers insist, was undoubtedly Tyburn. 'The Elms' is mentioned in Chronicles of the reigns of Edward I and Edward II, although this term has been used for both The Elms at West Smithfield, as well as The Elms at Tyburn. The sentence ordered that Wallace's head should be exposed on London Bridge. This is the first recorded instance of a severed head having being exposed there. His quartered body was displayed in Newcastle, Berwick, Perth and Stirling. In 1306 there were two further executions of Scottish leaders. On 7 September Symon Frisel (Fraser), was hanged as a thief, beheaded as a murderer, then the body was hung on a gibbet for twenty days before it was burnt. The head was fixed on a pole upon London Bridge, near the head of Wallace. On 7 November, the Earl of Athol, who claimed to be of royal lineage, was executed. Edward I said of him, 'If he is of nobler blood than the other parricides, he shall be hanged higher than they.' Lord Athol was brought to London and condemned at Westminster. Then, as he was of royal descent, instead of being drawn to the place of execution, he rode on horseback. He was hanged on a gallows fifty feet high. Then let down, half alive, so that his torment might be the greater, very cruelly beheaded (the chronicler does not say exactly how this was done), then the body was thrown into a fire, that had previously been kindled in sight of the sufferer, and reduced to ashes. The head was placed on a spike on London Bridge but higher than the other 'traitors', in regard to his royal descent.

Quartering of An Embezzler 1377

He was first drawn most uncomfortably to the place of execution …

In April 1377, Sir John Menstreworth was executed at Tyburn, having being found guilty of embezzlement. Sir John had embezzled large sums of money entrusted to him by no less a personage than the King (Edward III) himself, for payment of His Majesty's soldiers in France. The traitorous knight had fled to Pamplona in the kingdom of Navarre, where he was captured and brought back to London. He was first drawn most uncomfortably to the place of execution, then hanged and afterwards he was cut down and his body was divided into four quarters and sent to four principal cities in England. Sir John's head was placed on a pike on London Bridge, where it remained for 'a long time'.

Monks Suffer at Tyburn 1535

… these blessed fathers be now as cheerfully going to their deaths as bridegrooms to their marriage …

On 18 June 1535, three monks of London's Charter House, named Thomas Exmew, Humphrey Middlemore and Sebastian Newdigate, were drawn to Tyburn, hanged and quartered, for denying the King's supremacy. Sir Thomas More (1478–1535), distinguished statesman and scholar (canonized 1935), himself shortly to be executed, in July, for similar reasons (in his case he was beheaded and spared any mutilation, at the express command of the King, because he had held the highest office in the land. His execution shocked educated Europe), saw them from his cell, being taken out of the Tower and said to the lieutenant of the Tower's wife:

> *Lo, dost thou not see, Meg, that these blessed fathers be now as cheerfully going to their deaths as bridegrooms to their marriage? Wherefore mayest thou see, mine own good daughter, what a great difference there is between such as have in effect spent all their days in a strait, hard, penitential and painful life religiously, and such as have in the world, like worldly wretches as thy poor father has done, consumed all their time in pleasure and ease licentiously. For God, considering their long continued life in most sore and grievous penance, will no longer suffer them to remain here in this vale of misery and iniquity, but speedily hence taketh them to the fruition of his everlasting deity. Whereas thy silly father, Meg, that like a most wicked caitiff hath passed forth the whole course of his miserable life most sinfully, God, thinking him not worthy so soon to come to that eternal felicity, leaveth him here yet still in the world, further to be plunged and turmoiled with misery.*

Murder and Mutilation in Long Acre 1687

She was found guilty of petty treason and sentenced to death.

In 1687, Mary Aubrey, a midwife, murdered her husband and chopped off his head and limbs, in Long Acre, Covent Garden, assisted by her young son. She was found guilty of petty treason and sentenced to death. A verdict of petty treason, considered more serious than murder, was established when any person out of malice took away the life of

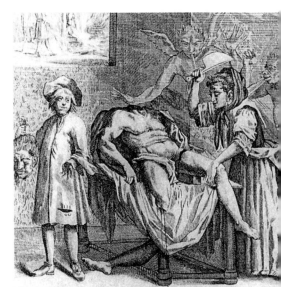

Mary Aubrey dismembering her husband's body, assisted by her young son, in 1687. Her hanging and burning at Tyburn is depicted top left. Author's collection

someone to whom he or she owed special obedience. For instance, as in this case, a wife murdering her husband, or a servant killing his or her master or mistress, or an ecclesiastic his superior. However, a wife's accomplices in the murder of a husband would not be guilty of petty treason. Mary Aubrey was hanged and then burned at Tyburn. Her son was acquitted as he was considered to have only acted under his mother's coercion.

A Fortuitous Reprieve 1705

He said the pain he felt in hanging was infinitely surpassed when his blood was recovering its usual course of circulation.

John Smith was condemned to die at the Old Bailey, on 5 December 1705 for burglary, he was convicted for breaking into shops in Leadenhall Market and stealing fifty pairs of shoes, one hundred and forty-eight pairs of gloves and twenty-two pairs of stockings. On 12 December 1705, he was conveyed from Newgate to Tyburn. James Montague in *The Old Bailey Chronicle 1700–83* writes:

After hanging five minutes and a quarter, a reprieve was brought … The malefactor was cut down and taken with all possible expedition to a public house where proper means was pursued for his recovery, and with so much success that the perfect use of all his faculties was restored in about half an hour.

There are some members of the criminal classes who simply do not seem to be able to mend their ways. Having survived this dreadful ordeal any reasonably minded person would have counted themselves extremely lucky and mended their ways. One would have thought Smith would not have wished to place his life in peril again, particularly when one bears in mind his own account of his experience on the dreaded 'Triple Tree'. Smith said that when he was first turned off he felt excessive pain, but that it almost immediately ceased. The last circumstance he recollected was like an irregular and glimmering light before his eyes. He said the pain he felt in hanging was infinitely surpassed when his blood was recovering its usual course of circulation. He was known thereafter as half-hanged Smith. John Smith found himself once again in the news. On 9 November 1706, it was reported:

The officers of her majesties guards yesterday drew out their companies in St. James's Park, which were viewed by Smith (sometime since hang'd at Tyburn, but reprieve coming was cut down before dead) and two other persons in masks, in order to discover felons and housebreakers: out of which 2 serjeants with 6 soldiers were seized as criminals and committed to the Marshalsea prison.

Smith had received an unconditional pardon but it seems this habitual petty-criminal had no intention of reforming. Before long he was again tried for burglary but was acquitted on a point of law. He chanced his hand a third time and was again apprehended on a charge of burglary and committed for trial at the Old Bailey in April 1715, for breaking into a warehouse and the house of John Cooper. Once again, good fortune smiled on Smith. The prosecutor,

Half-hanged Smith, cut down from the gallows 12 December 1705. Author's collection

John Cooper, died before the trial and Smith was discharged. I have been unable to trace anything further about this three times lucky John Smith, other than it was said that he died at sea.

The Major Who Cheated the Hangman 1729

Swords could be heard clashing and a waiter broke open the door.

Major John Oneby had distinguished himself as an officer in the Duke of Marlborough's military campaigns. He was described in contemporary accounts as a swaggerer and a bully. He had also gained a somewhat sinister reputation as a duelist, and had twice killed rivals, in duels in Bruges and in Jamaica. Following the signing of the treaties of the Peace of Utrecht in April and July 1713, the Major was placed on half pay. In order to supplement his reduced army pay, he turned to gambling, at which he became a professional, and was said to have been seldom without cards or dice in his pocket. Major Oneby was known for his quick temper and his fellow gamblers knew it was wiser not to pick a quarrel with him. However, one night in 1727, Oneby fell out over a bet, with a Mr Gower, in the *Castle Tavern*, Drury Lane. He threw a decanter at Gower, who returned the compliment by throwing a glass at Oneby. Swords were drawn but after the intercession of their fellow gamblers, were put up again. Although Mr Gower was keen to make the peace, the Major was in a different frame of mind altogether and swore to 'have his blood', a threat clearly heard by all present. When the party broke up, Major Oneby called Mr Gower into a private room and shut the door. Swords could be heard clashing and a waiter broke open the door. As the assembled company rushed into the room, the Major, with his sword in his right hand, was holding Mr Gower up with his left. Gower's sword was laying on the floor and a bloodstain, ever increasing in size, could be seen on his waistcoat, as blood gushed from a wound in his abdomen. Someone called out:

You have killed him!

To which Oneby replied:

No, I might have done it if I would, but I have only frightened him.

The Major was not correct in this assumption, as Mr Gower died the following day from the wound he had inflicted upon him. Mr Gower's death resulted in Major Oneby's arrest and incarceration in Newgate. A month later he was tried at the Old Bailey. However, the jury, other than agreeing that the Major had instigated the quarrel and had not denied he had killed Gower, were unable to agree upon the exact measure of guilt. This resulted in a special verdict being given, which would require further consultation with the judge and eleven other judges debating the issue. Major Oneby hoped to secure a manslaughter verdict. He was remanded in Newgate until his case could be heard. Justice, however, was slow on this occasion, as for a further two years, the Major remained in Newgate, and growing impatient, he prayed the Court of King's Bench that counsel might be heard in his case. Major Oneby was brought into court before the Lord Chief Justice Raymond and arguments were heard by both sides. Judgement was reserved until the judge had consulted his eleven brethren. The Major was confident of his acquittal and on the journey back to Newgate entertained his friends in the *Crown and Anchor Tavern*. He continued to be in high spirits for the next few months whilst waiting in Newgate for the result of the judges' conference. The twelve judges met in Sergeant's Inn Hall, and counsel was heard on both sides. The deliberations lasted an entire day. That evening a friend called to see the Major, who was enjoying a bowl of punch. The news he bore was bad. He told the Major that eleven of the judges had decided against him. The next day, Mr Ackerman, the keeper of Newgate, came to put irons on the Major, unless he was prepared for a special keeper to occupy the same room. The Major engaged the services of one John Hooper, later to become the public executioner, as his personal keeper. He spent the remainder of his days in fruitless efforts attempting to get his friends and relations to secure him a pardon but the threat that he would have Gower's blood had weighed greatly against him. He spent his time laughing at the jokes of Hooper or in fits of rage against those he considered to have deserted him in his time of need. When news of his imminent execution came, the Major wrote his will:

> *Cousin Turvill, give Mr. Ackerman, for the turnkey below stairs, half a guinea, and Jack Hooper who waits in my room five shillings. The poor devils have had a great deal of trouble with me since I have been here.*

The Major was to die on the Monday. On the Saturday night before execution, on learning that a petition for his pardon had been rejected, he resigned himself to his fate. When a friend called to see the Major at about seven in the morning, he called out to his servant, 'Philip, who is that?' When Philip entered the Major's cell, he discovered the prisoner bleeding profusely from a deep gash to the wrist. The Major died before a surgeon could be called.

Execution of a Miniaturist 1761

> *… he told her she was a very impertinent woman, at which she struck him a violent blow on the chest.*

Theodore Gardelle was a Swiss painter, a specialist in miniatures, who lodged with Mrs King, on what would be today the western side of Leicester Square but was then known as Leicester Fields. An otherwise inoffensive man, he was goaded into a fit of frenzy by his landlady after she repeatedly poured scorn on a miniature portrait of her, which he had executed. Early in February 1761, Mrs King came into the parlour, which Gardelle used, a room which was *en suite* with her own bedroom, and began to verbally abuse him about the miniature. She had desired to have a particularly good portrait and she was not at all satisfied with his efforts. The quarrel continued from the parlour to the adjacent bedroom and Gardelle said that being provoked by her onslaught on him, he told her she was a very impertinent woman, at which she struck him a violent blow on the chest. He pushed her away from him, as he said at the trial:

... rather in contempt than anger and with no desire to hurt her.

Theodore Gardelle disposing of pieces of the body of his landlady, Mrs King. Author's collection

Mrs King's foot caught in the floor-cloth and as she fell backwards, her head hit a sharp corner of the bedstead with great force. As blood streamed from her mouth, Gardelle went to assist her. She pushed him away, with threats of charges of assault. The more he tried to pacify her, the more she threatened him, and afraid of being charged with a criminal assault, he completely lost his head and picked up a sharp pointed ivory comb, which lay on her toilette-table and drove it into her throat. As the blood gushed from her mouth and the wound to her neck, Mrs King continued to rant, until her voice gradually faded away and she died. Gardelle said he threw the bedclothes over her, and horrified at what he had done, fell away in a swoon. When he came round he examined the body to see if Mrs King was quite dead. On seeing her dead body and confused at what to do next, he staggered and hit his head on the wainscot, which raised a bump over his right eye.

There was only one other resident in the house, a maid-servant, and he had sent her out on an errand that morning. Another lodger was out of town, and his servant was also away. When she returned and found her mistress's bedroom door locked, Gardelle told her that Mrs King had gone to the country for the day. He later paid the girl her wages on behalf of Mrs King and discharged her. He told her that Mrs King intended to bring a new maid home with her from the country.

Having got rid of prying eyes, Gardelle set about trying to conceal his crime. He stripped the body and laid it out on the bed. He disposed of the bloodstained bedclothes by putting them in soak in a tub in the back washhouse. The servant of the absent lodger returned late that night and enquired after Mrs King. Gardelle said that she had not returned from the country and he would wait up for her and let her into the house. Next day he said that Mrs King had returned and gone away again early that morning. This went on from Wednesday to Saturday, with no suspicion that anything was amiss. Meanwhile, Mrs King's body lay on the bed. On the Sunday, Gardelle decided that he had better dispose of it. He began to dismember Mrs King, disposing of blood and some pieces of flesh in various sinks. He also burned some body parts. He laid other parts out in the cock-loft. Callers at the house continued to ask after Mrs King and Gardelle told them that he expected her any day. However, on the next Thursday, the bloodstained bedclothes were found in the wash tub. When Gardelle went to the washhouse and asked what had become of the linen he aroused suspicion and the discharged maidservant was found. She denied any knowledge of the contents of the wash tub. The neighbours began to make further enquiries. Mr Barron, an apothecary, came and questioned Gardelle, who gave such unsatisfactory answers that a warrant was obtained for his arrest. When the house was properly searched, conclusive evidence of foul play was discovered. Portions of the missing woman were found in the cock-loft and elsewhere in the house, and some jewellery known to have been Mrs King's was found in Gardelle's belongings. Gardelle, who had been taken to the New Prison at Clerkenwell, did not deny his guilt. At Clerkewell, he attempted to commit suicide by taking forty drops of opium. His attempt failed and he then swallowed twelve halfpennies, hoping that the verdigris would kill him. It did not but he suffered greatly from stomach pains. He was removed for greater security to Newgate, where he was closely watched. Theodore Gardelle was tried at the Old Bailey and found guilty of murder. He was hanged on a specially erected scaffold in the Haymarket near its junction with Panton Street, chosen as the most suitable spot nearest the place where he committed his crime. Gardelle passed Mrs King's house on his way to the scaffold. After his execution his body was taken to Hounslow Heath, where it was hanged in chains.

Slain by His Cousin, a Peer of the Realm 1765

Lord Byron's sword had penetrated Mr Chaworth's navel and made a wide gash in the stomach.

The story of the fifth Lord Byron's murder of his cousin, William Chaworth, has been well documented in the many volumes written about his more illustrious great-nephew and heir, the poet, George Gordon Byron, the sixth Lord Byron. Judging by the many accounts of the unsavoury exploits concerning William Byron, the fifth Lord, it is not without foundation that he was universally known as 'the Wicked Lord'. Lord Byron's country estate surrounded Newstead Abbey in Nottinghamshire. The Byrons were one of the oldest landed families in the county, having come over to England during the Norman conquests. Newstead was once completely surrounded by Sherwood Forest but by the eighteenth century, the forest was slowly retreating before the advance of tilled farms, villages and other large country estates, the finest and nearest of which was Annesley, the seat of the Chaworths. Annesley was joined to

Newstead by a long avenue of oaks, known as the 'Bridal Path'. The two families had been united by the marriage of the third Lord Byron with Elizabeth, daughter of Viscount Chaworth. In 1765 William Chaworth, of Annesley Hall, was the neighbour of his cousin, Lord Byron of Newstead Abbey.

These country landowners habitually went to London, where they gathered once a month at the *Star and Garter* tavern in Pall Mall. On 26 January 1765, the usual meeting took place and all went well until the talk turned to the best methods of preserving game. Mr Chaworth believed that poaching should be dealt with severely, whereas Lord Byron declared the best way to preserve game was to pay no heed to it. To add weight to his point that poaching should be stamped on, Mr Chaworth remarked, that he himself and Sir Charles Sedley, the owner of a neighbouring estate to Newstead and Annesley, had more game on five acres than Lord Byron had on all his manors. An addition to this statement angered Lord Byron very much. Mr Chaworth said if it was not for their precautions (his own and Sir Charles Sedley's), Lord Byron would no longer have a single hare on his land. Lord Byron asked where Sir Charles's manors lay and Mr Chaworth replied:

> *If you want information with respect to Sir Charles Sedley, he lives in Dean Street, and, as to myself, your lordship knows very well where to find me.*

With those words Mr Chaworth left the room. A little while later Lord Byron also left and found Mr Chaworth on the staircase. Words were exchanged and a waiter was asked to show them to an empty room. The waiter showed them to a room and closed the door as he left. A short while later a bell rang and the innkeeper went to see what was required. When he entered the room he found Lord Byron and Mr Chaworth at grips. Mr Chaworth was severely wounded. He was carried to his lodgings, where he died the next day. Before he died, Mr Chaworth said that he, himself had made the first thrust. A charge of murder was brought against his Lordship.

A peer accused of murder could only be tried by the House of Lords. Once preparations for a trial had been made, Lord Byron was invited to place himself in custody in the Tower of London. He was taken to his trial in Westminster Hall, by coach, escorted by mounted guards. The executioner's axe was placed before him with the blade facing towards him. The hall was packed and seats were being sold for six guineas each. A surgeon explained how Lord Byron's sword had penetrated Mr Chaworth's navel and made a wide gash in the stomach. He expressed the opinion that he had no doubt that this wound had been the cause of death. Lord Byron tendered his plea of Not Guilty. The fact that William Chaworth had drawn his sword first was in Lord Byron's favour. The customary vote was taken, starting with the peers most recently created and ending with the princes of the blood. Lord Byron was found Not Guilty of murder, but Guilty of homicide. Under a special statute affecting peers of the realm, Byron could plead benefit of clergy and this amounted to acquittal. A first offender who could read one verse of the Bible was declared to be under the jurisdiction of the Church and released from punishment from the temporal courts. As sentence was pronounced and the usher called out 'Oyez! Oyez!', the Lord High Steward snapped his white wand, and William, Lord Byron was set at liberty to return to his seat at Newstead. It was made clear, however, Lord Byron would not be made welcome in London again. He lived thereafter as a scandalous recluse with 'Lady Betty', a servant girl, as he had driven his wife away through his wicked ways. To his dying day on 21 May 1798, the Wicked Lord kept the sword with which he had killed his cousin hung on his bedroom wall.

An Infamous Forger and Swindler, Charles Price 1786

None of his accomplices or his agents knew his true identity, as they never saw him except in disguise.

When one particular prisoner incarcerated in Tothill Fields, Bridewell was found to have taken violent hands upon himself in January 1786, there were few who shed a tear for his departed soul. The prisoner's name was Charles Price, who was one of the most notorious forgers and swindlers of the eighteenth century, who preyed upon unsuspecting victims in both the City and the fashionable West End alike. Charles Price, otherwise known as Old Patch (so called from one of the many disguises he adopted while carrying out his nefarious

Charles Price c.1730–86. Author's collection

business), was born in London *c.*1730, the son of a clothes salesman, who despite the size and success of his enterprises, worked largely alone. He occasionally employed boys to pass his forged bank-notes but none of his accomplices were ever that close to him.

Price was a very clever and meticulous forger. He went to extraordinary lengths to avoid discovery. The banknotes he forged were produced with the utmost precision. He made his own paper, with the correct water-mark, engraved his own plates and even manufactured his own ink. He ran three homes. The first of which was his marital home. In the second, he installed a woman who helped him in his schemes and the third he transacted some of his money laundering business from, always in disguise. None of his accomplices or his agents knew his true identity, as they never saw him except in disguise. One of his favourite disguises was that of an infirm old man. He was:

> *... wearing a long black camlet cloak, with a broad cape fastened up close to his chin. With this he wore a big, broad-brimmed slouch hat, and often green spectacles or a green shade. Sometimes his mouth was covered up with red flannel, or his corpulent legs and gouty feet were swathed in flannel.*

His schemes to swindle unsuspecting victims were ingenious to say the least. On one occasion he devised a plan in which he was to 'expose a swindler'. In one of his disguises, he discussed the plan with a respectable city merchant, with whom he had become acquainted and had gained his trust. The swindler, none other than Price himself in yet another disguise, was by the design of his other persona, inveigled into the merchant's house in order that he could be 'given up to the police'. The swindler proposed that he should buy himself off for £500. The merchant, seeing the opportunity to make some easy money accepted his proposal and the money was paid with a thousand pound note, for which the swindler was given change. Naturally, the £1,000 note was one of Price's own forgeries.

Charles Price, disguised as 'Old Patch.' Author's collection

In another scam, in one of his disguises, Price engaged a boy. He dressed him in livery and sent him round the town to buy lottery tickets, always with large (forged) notes, for which change would always be required. This way he amassed considerable sums by passing off the counterfeits.

Price operated successfully over many years. The officials at Bow Street believed that the countless scams and swindles executed by Price were the work of a well organized gang headed by 'Old Patch', Price's most famous disguise. It was only after considerable time had been expended that any real leads put them on the right track. One of many endorsements upon a forged note was traced to a pawnbroker, who remembered the note had been given to him by a man named Powel, who sometimes transacted business there. A watch was placed on the pawnbrokers and when next Price turned up as Powel, on 14 January 1786, he was arrested. He was found to have on his person a large number of bank notes. He was held in Tothill Fields, until investigations could be made into his background. His natural appearance was described as:

> ... *a compact middle-aged man, inclined to stoutness, erect, active, and not bad-looking, with a beaky nose, keen grey eyes, and a nutcracker chin.*

At first, Price denied any knowledge of wrong-doing but as investigations into his background progressed and he realized all was up, when it became apparent that there was an overwhelming amount of evidence against him. He was found to be the man who in 1775 had advertised for a partner to provide capital for a planned brewery. He had been joined in this enterprise by the unsuspecting actor Samuel Foote, who was defrauded out of the profits and left to pay liabilities of £500. This very same man had started an illicit still, and had been arrested and sent to Newgate, until he had paid a fine of £1,600. He had, however, been fortunate on that occasion, as owing to the intervention of Foote and Lord Littleton, he had been released. This time however, it was clear there could be no such intercession. Rather than standing trial knowing at the end of it he would have to face the ultimate penalty, he decided to take matters into his own hands. He was found hanging behind the door of his cell, suspended from two hat screws, strengthened by gimlets.

During his vainglorious career as a forger and swindler, Price is believed to have defrauded individuals and banks out of as much as

£200,000 but how he disposed of his ill-gotten gains remained his secret. Despite his three homes, he did not live an ostentatious lifestyle in any of them, nor was he a drinker or gambler.

Murder of Lord William Russell 1840

... rather ill-looking, a baddish countenance; but his manner was calm though dejected and he was civil and respectful, not sulky.

What is today's Dunraven Street, running parallel with Park Lane and lying between North Row and Wood Mews, Mayfair, was, in 1840, when this premeditated murder took place, Norfolk Street. It was there, at No. 14, a small but elegant three-storied house, that Lord William Russell a seventy-three-year-old widower, lived with his staff of three servants; a cook, maid and valet, François Benjamin Courvoisier, who was Swiss. Lord William was by all accounts, an irascible, tetchy, somewhat peevish old gentleman, a younger son of the Duke of Bedford and uncle of the then Secretary of State for the Colonies.

On the morning of 6 May 1840, the housemaid, on coming downstairs from her quarters on the top floor, found the principal rooms in disarray. In the dining room, furniture had been turned upside down, the drawers of the escritoire were open and had been rifled, there was a bundle lying on the floor, as though thieves had been interrupted. It appeared that a burglary had taken place. She summoned the cook and they then called Courvoisier, who, much to their surprise came from his room already dressed. This was unusual in itself, because he was habitually late in the morning. Together they went upstairs to their master's bedroom. While Courvoisier opened the shutters, the housemaid on approaching the bed saw that Lord William was lying dead on his bloodstained bed. The quick-witted maid quickly took charge of the situation, and was given little assistance, if any, by either the cook, or Courvoisier. She rushed downstairs and out into the street and rang the bell of a house opposite. A footman eventually answered and she sent him to Hanover Square for the police. She sent another neighbouring servant to St James's, to summon Lord William's physician at 22 Cleveland Row.

Help soon arrived and despite the general mayhem elsewhere in the house, it was first assumed that Lord William had committed suicide. His throat had been cut from ear to ear, a towel had been placed over his face and this was soaked with blood, which also covered the pillows and bedding. There were no bloodstains anywhere else in the room, nor for that matter, were there any elsewhere in the house. However, it soon became apparent that this was no suicide, when it was discovered that some silver and other valuable items were missing and after further examining the evidence at the scene it was declared that suicide was impossible. It was clearly proved that no forcible entry had been made into the house. There were marks upon the door which had apparently been made from the inside, supposedly by a poker and chisel, later found in the butler's pantry, used by Courvoisier. The valet had attracted the suspicions of the police by his strange behaviour. He had hung over the body in an agitated manner, had not answered any questions or taken part in any of the proceedings. The police formed the opinion that the valet was more concerned about his own position than the tragic events. He kept repeating:

What shall I do? I shall never get another position.

Further suspicion was aroused by the bundle in the dining room, which contained small items of plate and jewels that a thief would normally have put into his pocket, leading those investigating the crime that the scene had been staged, but fortunately for them, not with any degree of expertise. In this the police were not wrong.

Investigations soon revealed the true extent of the situation. In his Lordship's bedroom a *rouleaux* box for sovereigns had been broken open. Likewise the jewel box and note case from which a ten pound note, known to have been in Lord William's possession, had been taken. His Lordship's watch was also missing. Further suspicion was aroused by the position of a book and a candle by the bedside. The candle was placed so that it could throw no light on the book, which happened to be a copy of the *Life of Sir Samuel Romilly*. The futile efforts of the real murderer to throw suspicion on burglars had been amply proved to the satisfaction of the police, who were convinced the culprit was from within the household. Courvoisier was taken into custody and the cook and maid placed under surveillance. Three days later a search of the butler's pantry provided further circumstantial evidence against the valet. Behind the skirting board there were several rings belonging to Lord William, also his Waterloo medal and the ten pound note. Elsewhere in the pantry was a split gold ring that his Lordship used for carrying his keys, a chased gold

key and his Lordship's watch. With sufficient
evidence against him Courvoisier was committed
for trial. Courvoisier was first held in Tothill
Fields prison, where he was visited by the
diarist Charles Greville, who gave the
following description:

> *… rather ill-looking, a baddish countenance;*
> *but his manner was calm though dejected and*
> *he was civil and respectful, not sulky.*

A subscription was raised from foreign
servants in London, to provide funds for his
defence. The trial opened at the Old Bailey on
18 June. Courvoisier pleaded not guilty. The
first day's proceedings were spent mainly
listening to the evidence given by the maid, the

François Benjamin Courvoisier.
Author's collection

cook and the police. It was on the second day of the trial, that a
prosecution witness gave evidence that placed Courvoisier firmly in
the frame, as far as the jury was concerned. Madame Piolaine, a
Frenchwoman, gave her evidence. She had, unbeknown to
Courvoisier, already been taken to Tothill Fields, where he had been
incarcerated and identified him. Louis Piolaine and his wife's cousin,
Joseph Vincent, ran a small hotel, the *Dieppe*, situated in Leicester
Place, a small turning which runs between Lisle Street and Leicester
Square. Several years before the murder Courvoisier had worked
there for about a month. Six weeks before the murder Courvoisier
had called on Madame Piolaine and a few days later returned with a
brown paper parcel which he asked her to look after for him. He told
her he would collect it but had not returned. When her husband read
about the murder case the parcel was opened and it was found to
contain items of silver belonging to Lord William Russell. The jury
had no difficulty in deciding upon a guilty verdict and Courvoisier
was sentenced to death. After he had been taken to Newgate
following sentencing, he admitted that he had been justly convicted.

He later made three written confessions, which vary considerably
in content and are somewhat confusing. He admitted that he had
killed Lord William on the night of 5 May. He said:

> *His lordship was very cross with me and told me I must quit his service.*
> *As I was coming upstairs from the kitchen I thought it was all up with*

me; my character was gone, and I thought it was the only way I could cover my faults by murdering him. This was the first moment of any idea of the sort entering my head. I went into the dining room and took a knife from the sideboard. I do not remember whether it was a carving knife or not. I then went upstairs. I opened his bedroom door and heard him snoring in his sleep; there was a rushlight in his room burning at the time. I went near the bed by the side of the window, and then I murdered him. He just moved his arm a little; he never spoke a word.

Courvoisier was only prevented from suicide by the vigilance of his captors and he said he intended to open a vein with a bit of sharpened stick, which had been taken away from him when his mattress was changed. The execution took place outside Newgate on 6 July 1840.

The Condemned Cell, Newgate Gaol, where Courvoisier languished during his last days. Author's collection

The executioner was William Calcraft. As well as an enormous crowd which had gathered outside the gaol, there was a gathering of distinguished guests inside. First came the sheriffs, the sheriffs, aldermen and city officials, Lord Powerscourt and other peers and Mr Charles Kean, the famous tragedian, who was following in the footsteps of his father, the celebrated Edmund Kean, who had similarly witnessed the execution of Thistlewood (see Cato Street chapter 10), with a view to his professional studies.

It was reported that:

As early as six a.m. the number assembled already exceeded that seen on ordinary occasions; by seven a.m. the whole space was so thronged that it was impossible to move one way or the other.

There is one final note to add to this particular case. Shortly before he was executed, Courvoisier admitted that he had committed the

The Debtors' Doorway, Newgate Gaol, outside which Courvoisier was executed. Author's collection

murder while stripped naked. This confession was corroborated by a gentleman, who said he had seen the figure of a naked man, carrying a lighted candle, through the landing window of the house opposite, at No. 14 Norfolk Street, on the night of 5 May. He had, however, kept his peace, as he had not wished to compromise the reputation of a lady, in whose company he found himself. The celebrated criminologist and theatrical producer H B Irving, son of the actor manager Sir Henry Irving, presented a play at the Queen's Theatre, Shaftesbury Avenue in November 1909. The play was based on these very events and was written by the dramatist Percival Landon and entitled *The House Opposite*.

A Cat Defends Its Mistress 1867

> *... such was the ferocity of the attack by her loyal pet, that her husband was obliged to implore her to take the cat away from him to save his life ...*

An unusual case was heard before Mr Knox at Marlborough Police Court, during the first week of July 1867, when George Amey of 12 Fitzroy Place was charged with assaulting his wife, Isabella, in her residence at 36 Tottenham Street. The married couple were estranged, the husband cohabiting with another woman in Fitzroy Place.

On Saturday 29th June, George Amey called at his wife's residence and after a few moments began to verbally abuse her. At the court hearing, Isabella Amey appeared to have been brutally knocked about. She told the warrant officer that her husband knocked her down, jumped on her, and then throwing himself on her, seized her by the throat, and attempted to strangle her. Meanwhile, while she lay on the ground, screaming and in terror of her very life, aid came from an unexpected source. A favourite cat, named Topay, sprang at Amey and fastened her claws in his eyes and her teeth in his cheek. Mrs Amey added that such was the ferocity of the attack by her loyal pet, that her husband was obliged to implore her to take the cat away from him to save his life, as he was unable to do so himself. Mrs

George Amey attacks his estranged wife Isabella at her home at 36, Tottenham Street. Topay, her cat, springs to her aid. The Illustrated Police News

Amey, having removed the cat from her husband's face, was rescued from any further ill treatment, as her husband fled the scene.

Having ascertained from several witnesses to his satisfaction, that George Amey had been in the habit of ill-treating his wife, Mr Knox sent Amey to prison for one month. Comments were later made at the magistrate's leniency for what was a particularly brutal attack.

Butchered in Charlotte Street 1917

… a large number of wounds had been inflicted by a far weaker hand than the powerful brute of a man Voisin.

On 2 November 1917, a road-sweeper was at work in Regent Square, Bloomsbury. As he busied himself with his brush and shovel, he noticed that just behind the iron railings in the shrubbery of the central gardens, was a large parcel covered in sackcloth. He went into the gardens to investigate. He removed the parcel from the shrubbery and opened it. Inside he discovered to his horror, wrapped in a bloodstained sheet, and dressed in delicate lace underwear, the headless torso of a woman. On a paper wrapper was scribbled the misspelt message 'Blodie Belgiam'. Nearby, wrapped in brown paper, was a second parcel and this contained the woman's legs. There was one clue that was to prove crucial in the identification of the remains. On the bloodstained sheet in which the torso had been wrapped, was an embroidered laundry mark 'II H'. It was established that the remains had been dismembered by someone who had some knowledge of anatomy, and the time of death was established as being within the previous two days.

Chief Inspector Frederick Wensley was placed in charge of the case. The usual rounds of launderers were instigated and eventually the laundry mark was tracked down to a house in Munster Square, situated off Albany Street, Regents Park. At No. 50 a young Frenchwoman lodged. Thirty-two-year-old Emilienne Gerard had been missing from her rooms since 31 October. A search revealed an IOU for the sum of £50, signed by Louis Voisin. There was also a framed photograph, which later proved to be of Louis Voisin, who was discovered to be her lover.

Voisin was traced to the basement flat at 101 Charlotte Street, Fitzroy Square. When the police called there, Voisin was in the company of Berthe Roche, who apparently lived with him. They also discovered that his trade was a butcher. As Voisin spoke hardly any

English, it was decided to conduct the interview through an interpreter and Chief Inspector Wensley had them brought to Bow Street for questioning. There it was established that Voisin had known Emilienne Gerard for about eighteen months and an intimate relationship had developed between them. On 31 October they had met to say their goodbyes, on the eve of Madame Gerard's departure for France. She was going to see her husband who was a cook in the French army. For the moment all that had been established was the fact that Voisin and Madame Gerard were lovers. It had not at that point been established that the dismembered remains were actually those of Madame Gerard. Nevertheless Voisin was detained at Bow Street overnight.

The following morning, through an interpreter, Chief Inspector Wensley asked Voisin if he would mind writing out the words 'Bloody Belgium'. Louis Voisin was a hulking brute of a man, who had great strength but little intelligence. He laboriously wrote down the words five times. The last effort was strikingly similar to that written on the parcel. On seeing this, Chief Inspector Wensley was confident that he was on the right track.

After a further visit to Charlotte Street there was no doubt at all as to whose remains had been discovered in the parcels found in Regent Square. The kitchen contained the tools of Voisin's trade. As well as saws and knives hanging on the walls, there was also a big knife-sharpening wheel. The walls of the kitchen were spattered with blood. This proved to be human. An earring was found caught in a towel. It was later established this belonged to Madame Gerard. Further searching revealed even more damning evidence. In a little arched recess in the coal cellar the police found a cask of alum which also contained Madame Gerard's head and hands. Voisin owned a pony and trap. The trap was covered with blood. When questioned about the discoveries, Voisin said:

I went to Madame Gerard's place last Thursday at 11am, and when I arrived the door was closed but not locked. The floor and carpet were soaked with blood. The head and hands were wrapped up in a flannel coat that is at my place now. They were on the kitchen table. The rest of the body was not there. I was so shocked by such a sight I did not know what to do. I remained there five minutes stupefied. I did not know what to do. I thought someone had laid a trap for me. I started to clean up the blood and my clothes became stained … Then I went back to my place and had lunch, and later returned to Madame Gerard's flat and took

*the packet back home. I had no intention to harm Madame Gerard.
Why should I kill her?*

However, his story did not tally with the evidence and what Voisin
had intended to be a false clue, to suggest a xenophobic antiwar
motive, served only to trap him. Semi-illiterate, and not at all bright,
he was clearly unaware of the misspelling of what he had intended to
read 'Bloody Belgium'. His inability to spell, in part, proved to be his
downfall.

The theory put forward by the eminent Home Office pathologist
Bernard Spilsbury based on the evidence provided by the wounds to
the body, was that a large number of wounds had been inflicted by a
far weaker hand than the powerful brute of a man Voisin. However,
what the police believed may have happened was never admitted by
Voisin or Roche. This theory or at least something very like it, seems
the most likely explanation, based on the known facts.

On the night of 31 October 1917, London suffered one of the
worst Zeppelin raids. It is believed that Emilienne Gerard was in the
vicinity of Charlotte Street that night, and in fear of her life, she

The Murder of Madame Emilienne Gerard by Louis Voisin and Berthe Roche. The
Illustrated Police News

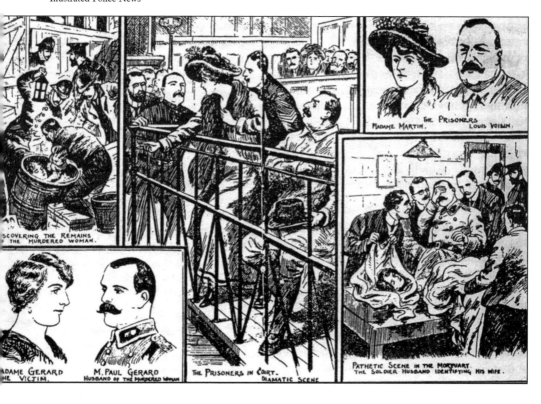

called at her lover's home seeking shelter and comfort from the raids. However, her lover was entertaining another lady friend who had until that point been unaware of Madame Gerard's existence. An ugly argument ensued, things got out of hand and Voisin and Roche killed Madame Gerard.

Voisin's trial before Mr Justice Darling, at the Old Bailey, was only remarkable for the fact that after being found guilty of murder, the judge pronounced sentence of death in French. Louis Voisin was hanged at Pentonville on 2 March 1918.

Berthe Roche was tried separately before Mr Justice Avory on 1 March 1918. She was acquitted of murder but charged as an accessory. The jury found her guilty and she was given a seven year prison sentence. However, she didn't serve it, as within a very short time she was certified insane. She died on 22 May 1919.

Murder After a Game of Bridge 1922

> *... there was blood on Lady White's unrecognizable face, blood on the sheets, on the walls and on the carpet.*

In the Spring of 1922, eighteen-year-old Henry Jacoby took the position of pantry boy at the *Spencer Hotel,* in the heart of the West End. Before he had been there a month, young Henry decided to avail himself of some of the wealthy residents' property. With robbery in mind, on the night of Monday 13 March 1922, he put his plans into action. The *Spencer Hotel,* a private hotel (now the *Mostyn Hotel)*, was situated in Portman Street. It was a comfortable hotel, dignified and quiet, the kind of hotel where retired people of good standing could spend the remaining years of their lives, being well taken care of, in pleasant surroundings.

One of the residents was sixty-year-old Lady White, widow of Sir Edward White, a former Chairman of London County Council. Alice Jane White, daughter of Captain C J Adams of Yeovil and Jersey, became the second wife of Edward White in 1893. Her husband died in 1914, leaving her well provided for. That evening, Lady White had been playing bridge in the drawing room. She had been at the hotel since the previous November. The forty or so other guests liked her and as Lady White received the domestic attention she required, the *Spencer Hotel* evidently suited her. One of Lady White's fellow guests, Mrs Adelaine Grainger, described the evening:

On Monday last, I was one of a small party who played bridge with Lady White. We were not playing for money. We stopped playing just before eleven o'clock. Lady White and I sat before the fire in the drawing-room, just next to the bedroom of Lady White, for about ten minutes. Then she went to her bedroom, and I went with her. I offered to carry her chair, and that was why I went with her, because I thought she looked pale and tired. It was a bedroom chair which she had taken from her room as there were not enough in the drawing-room. When she reached the door of the room I gave the chair to her. She turned on the electric light, and I then bade her good-night.

At five past eight on the morning of the 14 March, chambermaid Sarah Ann Pocock went into Lady White's room, Room No. 14, as part of her usual routine. The room was in semi-darkness, as the curtains were drawn:

I put a can of hot water in the basin of the wash-stand, and then looked at Lady White. I thought she had a red veil over her face.

She pulled the blinds at one of the two French windows. As she turned towards the bed, she noticed that there was no red veil but there was blood on Lady White's unrecognizable face, blood on the sheets, on the walls and on the carpet. Sarah did not panic. She went quietly downstairs and told the housekeeper of her discovery. A doctor was sent for and the police were called. Divisional Detective-Inspector Cornish, of New Scotland Yard, headed the investigation. Lady White was badly injured with serious head injuries. Police Division Surgeon, Dr Percy Bertram Spurgeon, was called to the hotel and found Lady White still breathing. She had an extensive fracture of the skull. The bone had been splintered and brain matter and blood clots were protruding. There was a laceration about eight inches long across the scalp and the edges were gaping. He concluded that the injuries were caused by more than one blow with a blunt instrument and that Lady White must have been rendered unconscious by the first blow. There was also an injury to Lady White's left hand. There were no signs of a struggle and no traces of forced entry. Lady White died during the early hours of the following morning. She never regained consciousness.

On the night of the murder pantry-boy Henry Jacoby told the porter he had heard some men whispering outside his basement room. However, nothing untoward was found and the porter returned to his duties, and young Henry to his bed. Next morning Lady White was found with terrible injuries in Room 14.

The inquest was opened at Marylebone Coroner's Court, by Mr H R Oswald, on 16 March. Meanwhile, police enquiries were continuing. Young Henry's all too eager enthusiasm to help, and his theories as to how the murder might have been committed, along with his tale of hearing men whispering outside his room, threw suspicion his way. When his room was searched, two blood-stained handkerchiefs were found. Henry caved in and told the police what had happened. Robbery was the motive. He left his basement room in the middle of the night. He took a hammer from a workman's toolbag, as repairs were being carried out at the hotel, then went a circuitous route through the kitchens to the guests' bedrooms. He had no specific plan in mind other than robbery, and it seems he tried another bedroom door first, which was locked, before trying Lady White's, which was not. He entered the room and before he had the chance to steal anything, Lady White woke up. He saw her in the beam of his torch, panicked and hit her with the hammer. In evidence Jacoby said:

> I struck her at least twice, because after I struck her the first time I heard her moaning and struck her again.

He then fled the scene and on returning downstairs, wiped the hammer on two handkerchiefs, before replacing it in the toolbag.

Jacoby was brought before Mr Leycester at Marylebone Police Court on 21 March. As he entered the dock of the crowded court, the collar of his overcoat was turned up and he carried a soft hat. His manner was casual and he seemed unconcerned. After evidence had been given by Inspector Cornish and others, Jacoby was remanded. The trial of eighteen-year-old Henry Julius Jacoby opened on 28 April at the Old Bailey before Mr Justice McCardie. Mr Perceval Clarke, Mr H D Roome and Mr W

Henry Jacoby who murdered Lady White in her hotel bedroom. Author's collection

The Mostyn Hotel *(formerly the* Spencer Hotel*), where the murder of Lady White took place, seen here in September 2005.* The author

Bentley Purchase acted on behalf of the Crown and Mr Lucian Fior for the defence.

The evidence having been presented, the jury consulted for some time in private, then returned to the court and the foreman said they were all agreed that Jacoby went into the room without intending to murder, but for the purpose of robbery. They wanted to know whether, bearing this in mind, they could bring a manslaughter verdict. Mr Justice McCardie said, that if Jacoby went into the room for the purpose of stealing, then the next question was, did he strike Lady White intending either to kill or inflict grievous bodily harm? Yet inasmuch as the victim had died from the injuries inflicted by Jacoby, he would be guilty in law of murder.

The jury brought in a guilty verdict, but with a strong recommendation to mercy on account of his youth and because they did not believe he entered the room with the intention of killing. Asked if he had anything to say, Jacoby replied:

Nothing at all, sir.

Sentence of death was then passed on the prisoner but the judge declared he would forward the recommendation to mercy to the Home Secretary. Despite this, there was to be no reprieve and Henry Jacoby was hanged at Pentonville on 7 June 1922. In the Condemned Cell, Jacoby wrote several letters, one of which concluded:

H. J. 382 – please excuse this curious signature, as this is what I shall be buried under.

Gallant Death of a Field Marshal 1922

Sir Henry, drew his dress sword, the only weapon he had to defend himself with but was powerless against the assassins' bullets.

Field Marshal Sir Henry Wilson was assassinated by two English-born members of the IRA, both ex-servicemen, Reginald Dunn and Joseph O'Sullivan on the front doorstep of his Belgravia home at 36 Eaton Place, after returning home from unveiling the War Memorial at Euston Station. Sir Henry Hughes Wilson (1864–1922) was born in Edgeworthtown, County Longford, Ireland. After serving in Burma and the Boer War, he was commander of the Staff College (1910–14), rising to Chief of the Imperial General Staff from 1918 until 1922, when he left the army and entered politics. He was made a baronet in July 1919 and later became MP for North Down, Ulster. On 22 June 1922, confronted by the two assailants on his own doorstep, Sir Henry, drew his dress sword, the only weapon he had to defend himself with but was powerless against the assassins' bullets. As the two assassins were chased down Ebury Street, not an easy feat for O'Sullivan to

accomplish, as he had a wooden leg, they first seized a cab in order to escape, then a victoria (a four-wheeled carriage for two people, with a collapsible top), firing as they fled at their pursuers, they injured two policemen. However, they were stopped in their tracks and seized by the crowd. Had it not been for the swift intervention of the police, Dunn and O'Sullivan would have been lynched on the spot. Sir Henry was buried in the crypt of St Paul's Cathedral. Dunn and O'Sullivan were hanged at Wandsworth on 10 August 1922.

36, Eaton Place, where Sir Henry Wilson was assassinated on the doorstep. The author

Acquittal of a Socialite 1932

I'll teach you to arrest me, you bloody swine!

In the early hours of 31 May 1932, neighbours in William Mews, situated between Belgravia and Knightsbridge, heard a shot and when they went to investigate, could hear Mrs Barney at No. 21, sobbing and calling out,

Don't die, chicken, don't die!

The neighbours misheard Mrs Barney, the resident, as what she was actually saying was, 'Don't die, Mickey'. The neighbours, however, were used to being awakened by quarrels at No. 21. Twenty-seven-year-old Mrs Elvira Barney had already shocked her neighbours and polite society, when, after her husband left her, she set up home with her twenty-four-year-old lover, Michael Scott Stephen, ex-public schoolboy, who described himself as a dress designer, the son of a London bank manager. Stephen lived largely by sponging off wealthy women. Elvira Dolores Barney was the daughter of Sir John Mullens, a former government broker, whose London residence was a house in nearby Belgrave Square. Elvira and her lover belonged to the set known as the 'Bright Young Things', who lived carefree lives around London, and provided fodder for Evelyn Waugh in several of his early novels. The exploits that this set found themselves involved in were reminiscent of the characters of Wodehouse's Wooster novels. Although their exploits extended further than mere riotous parties and absurd practical jokes, to the depths of decadence and promiscuous sex.

When a doctor arrived at Williams Mews he discovered Michael Stephen had been shot dead. The police were called and a .32 Smith and Wesson revolver was found lying close to the body. There were two empty chambers. Mrs Barney said that herself and Stephen had been to a nightclub with guests from a cocktail party the previous evening. After they returned home they began to quarrel, and Stephen picked up her pistol to shoot himself. As she struggled to stop him the gun went off. On 3 June, Mrs Barney was arrested and charged with murder. Her reply to the police when told she was to be arrested was:

I'll teach you to arrest me, you bloody swine!

The trial opened at the Old Bailey on 4 July 1932, before Mr Justice Humphreys. The prosecution was led by Sir Percival Clarke and the defence by Sir Patrick Hastings. Mrs Barney stuck to her story that the gun had gone off accidentally and never wavered. She didn't change a word of her statement. Despite convincing evidence from expert witnesses as to the likelihood of the gun going off accidentally, when a fourteen pound force needed to be exerted to fire the trigger, her society lawyer Sir Patrick Hastings managed to get her off; even in the light of what her neighbours said; that late one night, Mrs Barney appeared naked at her bedroom window and fired her pistol at Stephen in the mews below, as she called out to him:

Laugh, baby, laugh, for the last time!

Elvira Barney did not survive long. On 13 December 1936, she went to Paris, after enjoying a night of revelry on Christmas Eve, she was found dead in her hotel room on Christmas Day. She died from natural causes, aged thirty-one.

Gordon Cummins 1942

… strangled on her divan bed with one of her silk stockings and her body cut and disfigured by a razor and a knife …

Twenty-eight-year-old, 5ft 7ins tall, serial murderer Gordon Cummins, horribly mutilated and killed four women in six days after picking up his unsuspecting victims in West End pubs and clubs in wartime London. This pleasant, good-looking, young serviceman found easy pickings when he selected older women, who were looking to have a good time. Born in New Earswick in North Yorkshire, Cummins was well educated but not industrious. He moved to London where before the war he worked in a laboratory. In 1936, he had married a theatre producer's secretary. He was called up in 1941 and joined the RAF, where he trained for the air-crew. In early 1942 he was billeted in St John's Wood, where his air force colleagues nicknamed him 'The Duke' on account of his phoney Oxford accent. On Saturday, 8 February 1942, Cummins left his RAF billet, went to visit his wife and borrowed some money from her. He then went to the West End.

The following morning, the body of Miss Evelyn Margaret Hamilton, a forty-two-year-old pharmacist, was discovered in the

Piccadilly Circus in the heart of the West End, where Gordon Cummins went to pick up his unsuspecting victims. Author's collection

doorway of a brick air-raid shelter in Montagu Place, W1. She had been strangled. There were no signs of sexual assault but her handbag had vanished, containing the sum of £80. Cummins repeated this pattern of taking money and small items of little value from his victims, which were found at his billet. On 10th February, an ex-actress and Windmill showgirl, Nita Ward (real name Mrs Evelyn Oatley), turned prostitute, was found almost naked and dead on the bed, in her flat at 153 Wardour Street. She had first been strangled, then her throat had been cut, and the lower part of her body crudely torn open with a tin opener.

On Thursday 13 February, another prostitute, forty-three-year-old Mrs Margaret Florence Lowe (known as Pearl), was found murdered in her flat, Flat 4, 9–10 Gosfield Street, W1. She had been strangled on her divan bed with one of her silk stockings and her body cut and disfigured by a razor and a knife, which had been left nearby. In the kitchen was a half empty bottle of stout. A crucial piece of evidence, as was later discovered, was the bottle had Cummins's fingerprints on it, from his left hand, and it had been established the murderer was left-handed, by the pressure exerted during strangulation, evident by the bruising he left on the necks of his victims. Chief Inspector Greeno, Detective Inspector Higgins and Home Office pathologist Sir Bernard Spilsbury were attending the scene, when news came of yet another murder.

Thirty-two-year-old Mrs Doris Jouannet (also known as Doris Robson) of 187 Sussex Gardens, Paddington, the wife of an elderly hotel manager, a naturalized Frenchman, who at the time of her murder was on duty at a West End hotel. Mrs Jouannet led a double life, working as a prostitute when her husband was at work. She was found in the flat she shared with her husband and had been killed during the early hours of that morning. She had been strangled by a scarf, which was still wrapped round her neck and slashed several times with a razor blade.

Later that evening, Cummins picked up Mrs Greta Heywood near Piccadilly and had a drink with her at the *Trocadero Hotel*. When Cummins became what Mrs Heywood described as 'unpleasantly forward', she decided to leave. However he followed her into the street and chased after her, eventually catching up with her in St Alban's Street, where he forced her into a doorway and tried to strangle her. Fortunately for Mrs Heywood, as she passed out, Cummins was disturbed by a delivery boy taking some bottles to the nearby *Captain's Cabin*. Cummins panicked and fled the scene, leaving his gas mask behind. It had his service number printed on the case. Cummins's involvement in the four cases was quickly established and items belonging to his victims were found in his possession.

The trial began at the Old Bailey on Monday 27 April 1942 before Mr Justice Asquith. The prosecutor was Mr G B McClure, KC. Cummins was defended by Mr John Flowers, KC. With overwhelming and conclusive evidence against him the trial ended the following day. The jury took just thirty-five minutes to find him guilty. Cummins was executed at Wandsworth on 25 June 1942. Cummins is believed to have committed at least one other murder. Police suspect that he strangled nineteen-year-old prostitute, Maple Church, in October 1941, as the pattern of the bruising corresponded with that of his other victims, indicating that the murderer was left-handed. The killer had also rifled her handbag.

The Have-a-Go Hero, Charlotte Street 1947

I'm alright ... stop them ... I did my best.

A little after 2 pm on 29 April 1947, father of six, Alec de Antiquis, a thirty-four-year-old mechanic who ran a motor repair shop in Colliers Wood, South London, was in the West End on business, when he saw a robbery in progress at Jay's Jewellers, situated at 73–75 Charlotte Street. As he tried to foil the robbery at the junction of Tottenham Street by driving his motorcycle in front of the fleeing three masked raiders, one of the gang shot him through the head. A surveyor, Charles Grimshaw, also tried to stop the thieves fleeing but he was knocked to the ground and kicked. Mr Antiquis, shot in the left temple, slumped over in the gutter. As he lay dying, the three robbers disappeared among the crowds and traffic. An ambulance and police arrived within a few minutes.

The investigation was led by acting Superintendent Robert Fabian (who became a television celebrity after his retirement, with the programme *Fabian of the Yard*), assisted by Detective Chief Inspector Higgins and Detective Inspector Hodge. Fabian was quickly on the scene and as Mr de Antiquis was being lifted into the ambulance, heard the dying hero utter:

I'm alright ... stop them ... I did my best.

Mr Antiquis died in the ambulance before he reached hospital. It was established that the bullet that killed Alec de Antiquis was fired from a .32-calibre revolver. The gun, with five bullets still in the chamber, was discovered by an eight-year-old schoolboy, on the bed of the River Thames at Wapping, at low tide. This was tested by firearms' expert Robert Churchill, who had given expert evidence at many high profile shooting trials, including the famous Fahmy case of 1923 (see chapter thirteen), who confirmed it was the murder weapon. A .555 Bulldog revolver, loaded with six rounds, one of which had been fired, was also found, similarly discarded. The missing bullet was dug out of the woodwork in the jeweller's shop.

The attempted robbery itself had been a violent one. Sixty-year-old Albert Ernest Stock, a director had angered the robbers by shutting the safe door. One of them had beaten him about the head with a pistol. The assistant manager, seventy-year-old Bertram Thomas Keates had thrown a heavy wooden stool at one of the men, who pointed a gun at him and fired a shot, which lodged itself in the woodwork. The sound of the shot alerted people in the street and shouts of 'help' and 'murder' were heard. The three men panicked and ran into the street only to discover that a lorry had blocked the path of their getaway car, stolen for the purpose the previous day. They escaped on foot, but to add confusion to the events, many eye-witnesses believed they had escaped by car.

Statements were taken from twenty-seven people and descriptions issued of the wanted men. Two days after the shooting, a taxi driver, Albert Victor Grubb, turned up at Tottenham Court Road Police Station, and reported he had seen two men entering Brook House, 191 Tottenham Court Road, with handkerchiefs round their chins. When the police went to investigate, the discovery of certain articles of clothing in an empty room eventually led, after some very skilful detective work, to the arrest of twenty-three-year-old Charles Henry Jenkins (younger brother of Thomas Jenkins, involved in the killing of fifty-six-year-old retired naval commander Ralph Binney, run over following the robbery of a City jewellers, as he tried to stop the get-away car, on 8 December 1944. Jenkins was convicted of manslaughter and received eight years' penal servitude). Two of his friends were also picked up by the police, Christopher James Geraghty, aged twenty (who had been in borstal with Jenkins) and John Peter Rolt, aged seventeen, and both incriminated themselves. All three were charged with the murder of Alec de Antiquis on 19 May.

The trial of Geraghty, Jenkins and Rolt began at the Central Criminal Court, Old Bailey, on Monday 21 July 1947, before Mr Justice Hallett. It lasted a week. The prosecution was led by Mr Anthony Hawke. Geraghty was defended by Mr Wrightson, Jenkins by Mr Vick, KC, and Rolt by Mr O'Sullivan, KC. At the trial's conclusion, the jury took just fifty minutes to arrive at a guilty verdict in all three cases. Sentence of death was passed on Geraghty and Jenkins. Although it was Geraghty who fired the gun that killed Mr Antiquis, Jenkins was an accessory engaged in a joint enterprise of armed robbery. Rolt, who was too young to be hanged, was sentenced to be detained during His Majesty's Pleasure. Geraghty and Jenkins were hanged at Pentonville on Friday 19 September 1947 by Albert Pierrepoint. Ironically, on the day of the shooting Pierrepoint was walking down Charlotte Street on the way to meet some friends. He saw a lot of people gathered round a body in the road and continued on his way. There was a tremendous outcry at the executions, reinforcing the case of the abolitionists. Unfortunately, there was no such outcry at the lack of compensation that brave Alec de Antiquis's widow and six children received. Mrs Antiquis received a medal from the police commemorating her late husband's bravery, nothing else. After serving less than nine years, Rolt was released from prison on licence in June 1956.

The Murder of Mrs Elsie May Batten by Edwin Albert Bush, Cecil Court, 1961

... an eighteen-inch dagger was protruding from her chest.

In 1961, the shops in Cecil Court, a narrow walkway which straddles Charing Cross Road and St Martin's Lane, was then, much as it is today, occupied by mostly second-hand book, prints and curio shops. Seventy-two-year-old Swiss born, Louis Meier was the proprietor of an antique and curio shop situated at No. 23, run by his manageress Mrs Marie Gray. They were often away at auctions, so they had a part-time assistant, fifty-year-old, Mrs Elsie May Batten, who used to open the shop at about nine o'clock and put the displays of framed pictures outside. Mrs Batten travelled in each morning from her flat in Castletown Road, Fulham, and had been working at the little shop in Cecil Court for about two years. She didn't actually need to work, as she was comfortably off, being the wife of renowned sculptor Mark Batten, who was usually away from London four days a week, working in his studio at Dallington, near Heathfield in Sussex.

On the morning of Friday 3 March 1961, Mrs Batten kissed her fifteen-year-old daughter Griselda goodbye, before setting out for Cecil Court on the Piccadilly Line from Barons Court to Leicester Square. After unlocking the iron gates at 23 Cecil Court, and partially arranging the outside display, Mrs Batten was not seen alive again, except by her murderer. When Louis Meier arrived after midday to pay Mrs Batten's wages, he found that the usual outside display was incomplete and when he entered the shop, he saw the light was on but Mrs Batten was nowhere to be seen. It was only when Mr Meier went into the curtained-off area towards the back of the shop that he noticed Mrs Batten's legs sticking out from beneath the thick brocade curtain. As he drew back the curtain he discovered that Mrs Batten was dead and an eighteen-inch dagger was protruding from her chest.

23 Cecil Court, where Mrs Elsie May Batten was murdered, seen here in September 2005. The author

Detective Chief Superintendent John Bliss and Detective Superintendent Frank Pollard took charge of the case. Evidence at the scene suggested that a struggle had taken place. As well as the dagger in the chest, which had pierced her heart, there was also a wound to her neck, one to her shoulder and yet another to her back. She had also been hit over the head with a heavy stone vase, which was found nearby. Superintendent Pollard found a piece of board under Mrs Batten's body. On it was the print of the heel from a man's shoe.

A fifteen-year-old boy, Peter King, came forward to say he had called into the shop at 11.30 to buy a billiard cue. He saw the legs and hand of what he thought was a tailor's dummy, and finding no one around left. This established the time of death as being between 9am and 11.30 am. Mr Meier provided some vital information. He remembered that the previous day a young Indian-looking man had expressed interest in a dress sword costing £15 and also several daggers. He had returned later that day with a young woman. Police enquiries revealed that a young Indian man had called in to Robert's gun shop on the opposite side of Cecil Court and asked if they purchased ornamental swords. The following morning at about 10 am, the morning of the murder, the man called in at Robert's shop with a sword which he said he knew was worth more but was prepared to accept £10. The man had left the sword with the proprietor's son, Paul Roberts, but had not returned. This was the very sword which had inflicted injuries on the body of Mrs Batten.

From the descriptions of the man given by Mr Meier and the Roberts the police were able to use a technique for the first time in England, the Identikit picture. This relatively new technique had been successfully used in the United States for about eighteen months. It was the culmination of research carried out under the auspices of Hugh McDonald of Los Angeles Police Department. Although the concept of Identikit had been introduced to Scotland Yard in 1959, this was the first time it had been put to practical use. On the front page of every national newspaper this new tool in the fight against crime was used to catch Mrs Batten's killer. The jigsaw-like sections of the image had been assembled from the descriptions given. Along with the Identikit picture was a description of both the man and the girl who had accompanied him. On 8 March, PC Cole was on duty in Old Compton Street. He saw a young man who looked very similar to the Identikit picture. He was taken into custody and picked out in an identity parade. His name was Edwin Bush, a twenty-one-year-old Eurasian. The heel of one of Bush's shoes was an exact match for the heel mark found at the murder scene.

Bush's trial began at the Central Criminal Court on 12 May 1961. The judge was Mr Justice Stevenson. Bush was defended by Mr Christmas Humphreys, QC. To gain sympathy with the jury, Bush claimed in court that he had killed Mrs Batten after she had made a racist remark but this contradicted his earlier statement when he admitted that he had killed her to obtain the sword. He was found guilty of murder on 13 May. An appeal failed and he was hanged at Pentonville Prison on 6 July 1961.

Freddie Mills 1965

> *… family and friends believed he had been murdered, most likely as a warning to other club owners who resisted extortion.*

The celebrated and popular pugilist Freddie Mills was born in Parkstone, Poole, on 26 June 1919. During his successful boxing career, he was the world light heavyweight champion from 1948 to 1950. In the nineteen-forties, he invested some of his earnings in a Chinese restaurant at 143 Charing Cross Road, which, after operating successfully for a number of years, he eventually turned into a club, in the belief it would be more profitable. Although Mills wanted to create an entirely different atmosphere, like other similar clubs, it attracted elements from the seedier side of life. Mills was ever hopeful that the hostesses he employed there would not be 'on the game', as they invariably were at other clubs. The club was frequented by the notorious Kray twins. On 25 July 1965 Mills was found dead in his car in Goslett Yard, a court leading off the northern end of Charing Cross Road, close to his club. He had been shot with a shotgun, which lay beside him. Although the verdict at the inquest was suicide, Mills's family and friends believed he had been murdered, most likely as a warning to other club owners who resisted extortion.

Frankie Fraser in *Mad Frank's London*, mentions the Mills case in conjunction with a passage about the 'Jack the Stripper' case. The 'Nudes-in-the Thames', murders, as they were referred to in 1964, involved the murders of several prostitutes in West London, during 1964-5. They had been choked to death by their killer while they pleasured him with fellatio, evidence of this being provided by missing teeth (lost whilst struggling) and semen in the throats of the victims. Despite reports suggesting that the Stripper was a security guard at Westpoint Trading Estate, West Acton, where overwhelming evidence in a car spraying workshop linked the victims with flecks of paint found on the bodies, this did not stop a link, no matter how tenuous it might be, being made between the killings and Freddie Mills. Other commentators have mentioned Mills in conjunction with the Jack the Stripper case. Frankie Fraser says:

> ... *a married man from South London topped himself, leaving a note saying he was unable to stand the strain any longer.*
>
> *What is certain is that the killings stopped and the police put it about that this man was in fact Jack the Stripper. Then the rumours started, because it was about this time that the boxer Freddie Mills topped himself or got took out in Goslett Yard ... round the corner from where Freddie had a sort of Chinese Restaurant club. There was [sic] all sorts of stories about that. Some people said he did himself because the place wasn't doing well; that he was half gay and couldn't cope; that he was upset because he wasn't being used as a commentator for boxing on the radio no more; that he was being leaned on for protection and wouldn't pay, or that the Twins did him or that the Chinese Triads did him. Pick any theory you want.*
>
> *Then there was the story that he was the Stripper. The tale went that some coppers knew it and told him he had to top himself because they didn't want to have anyone arrest him ...*

What actually happened to Freddie Mills, described as a courageous and humane man, will probably never be known.

Lord Lucan 1974

A bent, bloodstained bludgeon, made of lead piping with an elastoplast grip, nine inches long and weighing two and a quarter pounds, was laying on the half landing of the basement stairway.

Thirty-nine-year-old Richard John Bingham, seventh Earl of Lucan, known as 'Lucky' to his friends, disappeared on the night of Thursday 7 November 1974, following an incident at his former Belgravia residence. At a little after nine o'clock that same night Veronica, Countess of Lucan, stumbled into *The Plumbers' Arms* in Lower Belgrave Street, with blood streaming down her face. That night the pub was quiet, with almost as many staff as customers. As Lady Lucan entered the pub she blurted out to the alarmed customers and staff:

Help me, help me. I've just escaped from a murderer ... My children ... my children ... He's in the house. He has murdered the nanny.

Lord and Lady Lucan had separated in January 1973. While she remained at the house in Lower Belgrave Street, with their three children and nanny, he moved into a basement flat nearby at 72a Elizabeth Street. By the time the police broke open the door of 46 Lower Belgrave Street, Lady Lucan had been taken by ambulance to St George's Hospital, Hyde Park Corner. In the basement breakfast room they found the battered body of the children's nanny, twenty-nine-year-old Sandra Rivett, stuffed in a US mail sack. A bent, bloodstained bludgeon, made of lead piping with an elastoplast grip, nine inches long and weighing two and a quarter

The Plumbers' Arms, *Lower Belgrave Street, where Lady Lucan went on the night of 7 November 1974 after being attacked.* The author

pounds, was laying on the half landing of the basement stairway. When Miss Rivett's body was examined by pathologist, Professor Keith Simpson, he found six splits in the head, severe bruising on both shoulders, caused by the bludgeon and other bruising which may have been defence wounds.

The Lucans' eldest daughter, Lady Frances, aged ten, made the following statement, which helps to pinpoint the course of events, by the timing of various television programmes which were being watched in the household that evening:

At 7.20 I watched Top of the Pops *in the nursery. Mummy, Camilla, George and Sandra were downstairs watching* The Six Million Dollar Man. *I joined them at 8.05 and we all watched*

46 Lower Belgrave Street, the Belgravia home of Veronica, Countess of Lucan and her children and their nanny, Sandra Rivett. The author

TV in Mummy's room. When the programme finished at 8.30 I went back to the nursery and played with my games. Sandra brought Camilla and George upstairs and put them to bed. I had had my bath and was wearing my pyjamas. I stayed in the nursery about five minutes. I went downstairs again to Mummy's room about 8.40. I asked Mummy where Sandra was and Mummy said she was downstairs making tea. After a while Mummy said she wondered why Sandra was so long. It was before the news came on at 9 p.m. I said I would go downstairs to see what was keeping her, but Mummy said no, she would go down. She left the bedroom door open, but there was no light in the hall. Just after Mummy left the room I heard a scream. It sounded as though it came from a long way away. I thought perhaps the cat had scratched Mummy and she had screamed. I was not frightened. I went to the door and called Mummy but there was no answer and I left it. At 9.05 the news was on TV and Daddy and Mummy both walked into the room. Mummy had blood over her face and was crying. Mummy told me to go upstairs. Daddy didn't say anything to me and I said nothing to either of them. I don't know how much blood was on her face. I didn't hear any conversation between Mummy and Daddy. I didn't see any blood on Daddy's clothes. I wondered what had happened but I didn't ask.

At 9.50 pm Lord Lucan telephoned his mother, the Dowager Countess of Lucan, at her flat overlooking Lord's Cricket Ground at St John's Wood. He told her that while passing the house he saw a stranger grappling with Veronica and had let himself into the house and fought him off, only to have Veronica think that he had attacked her. After asking his mother to pick up the children, he drove to friends in Sussex and told them the same story about seeing an intruder attacking his wife. He also wrote letters to other friends stating the same and declared his intention of 'lying doggo' for a while.

On Friday 8 November, Lord Lucan's car was found abandoned in Newhaven. In the boot was an empty US mail sack and a bludgeon

Entrance to 72a Elizabeth Street, the basement flat where Lord Lucan was living at the time of the murder. The author

made from the same lead piping as the one used to kill Sandra Rivett. Lord Lucan had disappeared, leaving no clues as to where he might have secreted himself. Despite numerous alleged sightings, all around the world, the missing peer's whereabouts remain a mystery.

Foul Murder of WPC Yvonne Fletcher, St James's Square 1984

A burst of automatic gunfire came from a first floor window.

In 1984, the dignified town house, formerly the home of Nancy, Viscountess Astor (1879–1964), the first woman to be elected to the House of Commons, at 5 St James's Square, was occupied by the

5 St James's Square, which was occupied by the Libyan People's Bureau in 1984, when WPC Yvonne Fletcher was shot. The author

Libyan People's Bureau. In April of that year anti-Gadaffi Libyans demonstrated outside the People's Bureau, against the Colonel's regime. The police were marshalling the rival factions in an attempt to prevent them clashing, by placing metal barriers at strategic points. On Tuesday 17 April, a burst of automatic gunfire came from a first

floor window. Several anti-Gadaffi demonstrators were injured and WPC Yvonne Fletcher, who was on crowd control duty, was killed outright. Her colleagues recovered her body and the square was sealed off. For four days WPC Fletcher's hat lay in the gutter where it had rolled. The diplomatic status of those responsible for murdering WPC Fletcher meant that the occupants of the Libyan People's Bureau were flown back to Libya. A memorial to the fallen policewoman was erected at the spot where she fell, the first such monument of its type.

The memorial to WPC Yvonne Fletcher, erected at the spot where she fell in St James's Square. The author

CHAPTER 2

Gunpowder Treason and Plot
1605

A watch, slow matches and touchwood, were found upon his person and a dark lantern with a light in it was discovered in a corner, presumably in readiness to light the fuses.

The Gunpowder Plot was the reaction of a group of Catholic gentlemen to the bitter disappointment of failing to obtain relief from the anti-Catholic laws. The conspirators, of which there were twelve, were recruited by Robert Catesby, a Warwickshire landowner of good family, who recruited Guido Fawkes (better known as Guy), from York. Guido Fawkes was born on 16 April 1570, the son of Edward Fawkes, an advocate and notary, who lies buried in York Minster. He died when Guy was very young. Guy Fawkes was Protestant. His mother remarried and Guy was orphaned at eight. He was brought up by his stepfather, Denis Bainbridge, who if not a Catholic himself, brought Guy into contact

Conspirators in the Gunpowder Plot. Author's collection.

with important Catholic families and Guy quickly became a Catholic convert. He served in the Spanish army in Flanders, in the Spanish wars against the Dutch, where he gained a high reputation for courage, fidelity, resolution and secrecy.

Since the beginning of his reign in March 1603, James I had been put under pressure to grant greater Catholic toleration. This he was not prepared to do. In the belief that it would further their cause, the conspirators planned to blow up the King and members of both houses of Parliament at the state opening of Parliament on 5 November 1605. In May 1604 they rented a house adjacent to the Palace of Westminster and painstakingly dug a tunnel through to the cellars beneath the House of

King James I. Author's collection

Lords. A cellar was filled with barrels of gunpowder, which had been so positioned as to, when ignited, have devastating effect.

One of the conspirators, aware of the dreadful carnage that would result from the mighty explosion caused by such a large quantity of gunpowder, decided to warn his brother-in-law, a Catholic peer, Lord Monteagle, to avoid the state opening. The letter, said to be in an unknown hand, was received by Lord Monteagle on 26 October, it read:

My lord, out of the love I beare to some of youere frendz I have a caer of youer preservacion. Therefor I would advyse yowe as yowe tender youer lyf to devys some epscuse to shift of youer attendance at this parliament. For god and man hathe concurred to punishe the wickedness of this tyme. And thinke not slightly of this advertisement but retiere youre self into youre contri wheare yoiue maye espect the event in safti. For thowghe theare be no appearance of anai stir yet I ave [r] they shall recevue a terrible bloue this parliament and yet they shall not seie who hurts them. This cowncel is not to be contemned because it maye do yowe good and can do yowe no harme for dangere is passed as soon as yowe have burnt the letter. And I hope god will give yowe the grace to mak good use of it: to whose holy protection I commend yowe.

To the right honorable
The Lord Monteagle

Lord Monteagle alerted the Secretary of State, the Earl of Salisbury, to this intelligence that same night. He showed the letter to some of the Privy Council but they could make nothing of it. Lord Salisbury said he thought there might be something in it as the information seemed to correspond with some he had received from abroad, that the papists were preparing to deliver a petition for greater toleration, which would be so well backed that the King would be loth to refuse. It seemed like a veiled threat. However, as the King was out of London, it was decided to take no action until he returned. On being informed of the letter the King decided that some kind of plot was afoot to endanger himself and Parliament at the state opening. He ordered that a search of the House of Lords should be made but not until the night of the 4 November, the eve before the state opening. Shortly before midnight on 4 November, Sir Thomas Knevet led a search party. Guy Fawkes was discovered in the cellar, along with thirty-six barrels of gunpowder. A watch, slow matches and touchwood, were found upon his person and a dark lantern with a light in it was discovered in a corner, presumably in readiness to light the fuses. Fawkes was bound hand and foot and after the council had been summoned, they joined the King in his bedchamber and Fawkes was taken there. When the King asked him:

Why would you have killed me?

Seventeenth century engraving by Wenceslas Hollar of Westminster, from the River Thames showing Westminster Abbey, Westminster Hall and the Houses of Parliament. Author's collection.

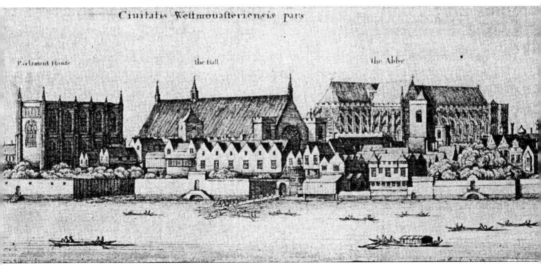

Fawkes replied:

Because you are excommunicated by the Pope.

Surprised by his reply the King enquired:

How so?

Fawkes replied:

Every Maundy Thursday, the Pope doth excommunicate all heretics, who are not of the Church of Rome; and you are within the same excommunication.

After a greater part of the night had been spent questioning him, Fawkes was taken to the Tower of London, where he was incarcerated in the vaults of the White Tower, which also contained the torture chamber, which was soon to be put to use. Meanwhile, several of the conspirators, including Catesby, were on their way to Warwickshire. Others connected with the plot were caught in *flagrante delicto* and

arrested. The plot having being discovered, Catesby was unable to summon help from his brother Catholics and decided to make a last stand at Holbeach, along with his fellow conspirators who had fled with him, as Sir Richard Walsh, High Sheriff of Worcestershire, closed in on them with three hundred men. In the last desperate fight Catesby was killed and those conspirators that survived were brought to London.

The King himself wrote the warrant permitting torture, allowing Fawkes to be tortured gently at first and then *et sic per gradus ad mia tenditur* (and so on step by step to the limit), and in the days and

The arrest of Guy Fawkes. Author's collection

weeks that followed Fawkes and other conspirators were shown no mercy as important information was extracted from them. The extent of suffering that must have been endured by Fawkes is no more clearly illustrated than by comparing his signatures before and after torture. One of the ringleaders, Francis Trensham, already seriously ill before his imprisonment and enduring much pain, died in the Tower, on 23 December 1605.

On 27 January 1606 the conspirators were brought by barge from the Tower of London to Westminster Hall, where they were arraigned before six earls, Lord Chief Justice Popham, the Chief Baron of the Exchequer, Sir Thomas Fleury, and Justices Walmis and Warburton. Sir Everard Digby was immediately separated from the rest as he pleaded

King James I hawking. Author's collection

guilty to the charges. The remaining seven pleaded not guilty to the long indictment, which attributed the Gunpowder Plot's origin to the Jesuits. The prisoners were not called upon to speak as it was considered there was no possible line of defence. While the jury was out, the Court began the trial of Sir Everard Digby.

Sir Everard made an admirable speech, which began by laying out his motives for his actions. He went on to make several requests. He said that as he alone was guilty, he alone should be punished and not his wife, nor any of his family. His son should inherit and his sisters should get that which was held in trust for them by himself. His final request was to ask pardon of the King and Court for his admitted guilt. He asked that his death would be sufficient punishment and that he might face death honourably by being beheaded. As the jury returned with a guilty verdict on the other seven, it mattered not what either Sir Everard or any of the others said. The same terrible sentence of half-hanging, unspeakable mutilation and exposure of the remains was pronounced.

After the prisoners had been condemned, they were taken back to the Tower by torchlight. Only two days were allowed for preparation to die. They were to be executed in two batches. Sir Everard Digby,

Robert Winter, John Grant and Thomas Bates, to be executed first in St Paul's churchyard and Ambrose Rokewood, Thomas Winter, Robert Keyes and Guido Fawkes, were to die the following day at Westminster. No reason was given for dividing the Winter brothers at their executions.

On the first day of the executions, 30 January, the prisoners were drawn upon sledges and hurdles to the western end of St Paul's churchyard. The City had gone to great lengths to ensure that the spectacle of the occasion would be an imposing one. The Lord Mayor issued instructions to the alderman of each ward in the City to ensure that one able person, with a halberd in his hand was standing in the doorway of every dwelling house that marked the route the prisoners would be drawn on their way to the scaffold. The men standing guard should remain there from 7 am until the return of the sheriff. Sir Everard Digby died first. The executioner was merciless. Sir Edward was cut down very quickly from his half-hanging and was fully conscious and alert during his public castration and disembowelling. The severing of the privy parts had been introduced during the reign of Elizabeth I, thought up by her supporters as an additional indignity inflicted on those who had conspired against her. He suffered the terrible ordeal with great bravery and was much admired by the crowd. Robert Winter deprived the crowd of any enjoyment as he rushed up the ladder and threw himself off, dying a swift death before any further indignities could be inflicted upon his live body, as death released him from any such pain. Grant too was rapidly dispatched. Before he died, Bates professed complete penitence. He said it was his love of Master Catesby that had caused him to forget his duty to God, King and Country.

On the next day, the remaining conspirators were dragged on sledges from the Tower to the old palace in Westminster, opposite the Parliament House. As the long procession passed through the Strand, Rokewood's wife, Elizabeth, watched from the window of her lodgings. As her husband passed by, he called out to her:

Pray for me.

His highly devout wife answered:

I will. Be of good courage and offer thyself wholly to God. For my part, I do as freely restore thee to God as He gave thee unto me.

The execution of the Gunpowder Plot conspirators, Old Palace Yard, Westminster. Author's collection

Winter was the first to be brought to the scaffold. He said very little but proclaimed he died a true Catholic. On the scaffold Rokewood firstly offended the crowd by praying God to make the King a good Catholic and secondly robbed them of their enjoyment by dying at what was to be his half-hanging before his butchery. Keyes came next and finally Fawkes, who was so weak with torture and sickness that the executioner had to assist him up the ladder. It was intended to inflict upon the man who was allegedly the greatest villain of them all, every torture that had been prescribed in the sentence to its full effect. He cheated the executioner and the crowd out of any pleasure they might have derived from seeing him suffer, as his neck was broken at once, and it was his dead body that the indignities were inflicted upon.

Such was the significance of the failure of the Gunpowder Plot that it was declared that 5 November should be a festival thereafter. The popular nursery rhyme, penned by a long forgotten hand has been recited down the generations to the present day:

> *Remember remember the fifth of November*
> *Gunpowder, treason and plot,*
> *I see no reason why gunpowder treason*
> *Should ever be forgot.*

The Thanksgiving Service for the deliverance of November 5 was not removed from the *Prayer Book* until 1854; and the anniversary which today we continue to celebrate on 'Bonfire Night', 5 November, with bonfires, effigies of Guy Fawkes and firework displays, was, until well into the nineteenth century marked with anti-Catholic demonstrations. In commemoration of the events of 1605, a search is still made of the cellars beneath the House of Lords on the eve of each state opening of Parliament, when ten yeoman of the guard conduct a search, carrying lanterns.

CHAPTER 3

Execution of Charles I
Whitehall, 1649

At the instant when the blow was given there was such a dismal, universal groan among the people as I never heard before and desire I may never hear again.

Andrew Broughton, the clerk of the court rose and read the sentence:

> *The said Charles Stuart, as a tyrant, traitor, murderer and a public enemy, shall be put to death by the severing of his head from his body.*

The King was visibly shocked by the sudden ending of the trial and his request to be allowed to reply was refused, he called out loudly to John Bradshaw, President of the High Court of Justice, 'Will you hear me a word, Sir?' Bradshaw replied, 'You are not to be heard after the sentence.' He ordered the guard to take the King away with the words 'Guard, withdraw your prisoner.' His Majesty called out 'I may speak after the sentence, by your favour, Sir. By your favour, hold! The sentence, Sir – I say, Sir, I do –' As the soldiers moved in to drag the King away, if necessary, His Majesty said resignedly, 'I am not suffered for to speak: expect what justice other people will have.' The King left Westminster Hall to shouts of Execution! Justice! Execution! As the King left some of the soldiers blew smoke in his face, when one cried out 'God bless you, sir!' the soldier was struck with a cane by an officer. During his trial, the King had been lodged in Cotton House, the Westminster home of Sir Robert Cotton. It was a handsome mansion with a garden running down to the River Thames, and conveniently situated near

John Bradshaw (1602–59), who presided at the trial of Charles I. Author's collection

Westminster Hall. Author's collection

Westminster Hall, a place easily guarded and one which could be safely cordoned off. However, on leaving Westminster Hall this final time, the King was hurriedly conveyed in a closed sedan chair along King Street to Whitehall Palace. Troops lined the entire route, all the while the sedan chair being watched by hordes of silent people from the street, windows and rooftops. The King entered the palace on foot through the Privy Garden, and between his guards he noticed a faithful old servant weeping. His Majesty said, 'You may forbid their attendance, but not their tears.'

The 150 Commissioners who had attended the trial and who were also responsible for deciding on a place of execution for the King and of ratifying his death warrant, opted for a site immediately outside the royal Banqueting House. *The Moderate,* a weekly newspaper that commenced publication during the summer of 1648, in its issue for 23–30 January, hailed their choice saying that this was the very place where Charles had first drawn his sword against his people:

> *The King's party, the day the citizens came down to cry for justice against Strafford, killed one of the citizens and wounded many, being the first blood spilt in this quarrel.*

The Trial of King Charles I, Westminster Hall, January 1649. Author's collection

However, in this *The Moderate* was inaccurate in its reporting of the events of May 1641, perhaps deliberately so. For when the London apprentices had massed outside Whitehall Palace, egged on by those parliamentarians who were rallying against the King's authority, in screaming for Strafford's (the King's chief minister) execution, the King's party did not retaliate. It was some seven months later during the Christmas revelries that the royal guards had clashed with some Puritan citizens, and although a few were injured, none had been killed. The choice for the King's place of execution had nothing whatever to do with the events suggested in *The Moderate*. The Commissioners' choice was purely a matter of convenience and security. This choice of a place of execution for the King is no better described than in Dame C V Wedgewood's description in *The Trial of Charles I*:

> ... *The open space before the Banqueting House was a great deal more easily guarded than the usual places of public execution, like Tower Hill or Tyburn. It was a relatively small square, overlooked on three sides by the buildings of Whitehall.*
>
> *The Palace of Whitehall extended about two hundred yards inland from its gardens and frontage on the river. The ancient thoroughfare called King Street that linked Westminster to Charing Cross was older than the palace, and no attempt had been made to close or divert this public way. It ran right through the precincts of the palace. Henry VIII had built the Holbein Gate over the street to carry a corridor linking the residential part of the palace on the riverside to the Tilt-yard, Cockpit and other additional galleries and outbuildings on the side of St James's Park. The new Banqueting house, with its stone façade in the classical Italian manner, was at right angles to the mellowed red and black chequered brick of the graceful turreted Holbein Gate. Opposite the Banqueting House, on the farther side of King Street, ran the blank wall of the Tilt-yard. The street was broad here, about a hundred and twenty feet, but every building that abutted on it was part of the Army Headquarters. Furthermore, during the war several windows of the Banqueting House had been bricked up, and a battery of guns had been mounted on a platform in the angle between the Holbein Gate and the Banqueting House. A better guarded part of the public street could not have been found.*

Of the 150 Commissioners who attended the trial, in the end just fifty-nine put their signature on the King's death warrant. Eleven years later, when the surviving signatories were put on trial for the murder of the King, it became evident that fear of Cromwell was one reason why some men signed the warrant. Three officers of the army were directed to see that the King was put to death between the hours of ten in the morning and five in the afternoon on Tuesday 30 January, these were Colonel Hacker, Colonel Hunks and Colonel Phayre.

King Charles 1. Author's collection

In the seven years since Charles had fled from Whitehall and the riots of the London apprentices, and in the ensuing years, the once beautiful Whitehall Palace had been ill used for its own purposes firstly by Parliament and later the army. As part of the defensive measures seven windows in the Banqueting House had been partially blocked by boards or masonry. The magnificent hall, with its great ceiling and its glorious paintings by Reubens, was barely visible in the dimly lit room. They showed the principal events of his father James I's reign, his own birth and his accession to the throne at his father's death. It was to be through this very hall, constructed with an entirely different purpose in mind, that the King was to walk on his way to the scaffold, which had been erected immediately outside. Built with high sides, which had been draped with black cloth to partially

obscure the view, its floor was level with the lower part of the windows on the first floor. The scaffold was 'L' shaped and had been built to fit the recessed addition to the main building, which was, when faced from King Street, to the left. It was there that a window had been removed and the hole enlarged, through which the king would pass.

Meanwhile, while the scaffold was being erected and

Bust of King Charles I, on the outside of the east wall of St Margaret's Church Westminster, facing Westminster Hall and the statue of Oliver Cromwell. The author

preparations made for the execution, the King was half a mile away in his apartments in St James's Palace. The House of Commons had granted the King's request to see his children, the eight-year-old Prince Henry, Duke of Gloucester and thirteen-year-old Princess Elizabeth. On the afternoon of 28 January they were brought from Syon House to St James's Palace and in the evening were taken to see their father. The other children had all escaped abroad. The Duke of Gloucester was a lively little boy, who on his few public appearances had

Syon House, from where the Royal children were brought to see their father on the eve of his execution. Author's collection

attracted a great deal of popular interest and applause from those who saw him. Rumours abounded that the King's enemies would put him on the throne in his father's place, as a puppet king, a possibility Charles was well aware of. Charles had had little to do with these particular children and had only come to know them at the end of the Civil War, as both had been in the hands of Parliament throughout the conflict. During the autumn of 1647 when he had been incarcerated at Hampton Court, they had visited him often. However, it had been fifteen months since he had last seen them. On seeing their father, both children immediately fell to their knees, Princess Elizabeth was crying bitterly. The King raised them to their feet and took them on one side, as the children had not come unaccompanied. He spoke firstly to his daughter, who was still weeping. He told her to listen carefully and to try to remember the important things he had to say. As the princess continued to weep, her father gently reproached her saying:

Sweetheart, you will forget this.

The princess replied:

No, I will never forget it whilst I live.

She did remember her father's words and what follows is Princess Elizabeth's own account of the King's last words to her, which she wrote down that night:

He told me he was glad I was come, and although he had not time to say much, yet somewhat he had to say to me, which he had not to another, or have in writing, because he feared their cruelty was such, as that they would not have permitted him to write to me. He wished me not to grieve and torment myself for him, for that would be a glorious death that he should die, it being for the laws and liberties of this land, and for maintaining the true Protestant Religion. He bid me read Bishop Andrews' Sermons, Hooker's Ecclesiastical Policy *and Bishop Laud's book about Fisher, which would ground me against Popery. He told me, he had forgiven all his enemies, and hoped God would forgive them also, and commanded us, and all the rest of my brothers and sisters to forgive them. He bid me tell my mother that his thoughts had never strayed from her, and that his love should be the same to the last. Withal he commanded me and my brother to be obedient to her, and bid me send his blessing to the rest of my brothers and sisters, with commendation to all his friends.*

The Princess added a postscript:

Further, he commanded us all to forgive these people, but never to trust them, for they had been most false to him and to those that gave them power, and he feared also to their own souls; and desired me not to grieve for him, for he should die a martyr; and that he doubted not but the Lord would settle his throne upon his son, and that we should be all happier than we could have expected to have been if he had lived.

To the little Duke of Gloucester, as he took him on his knee, the King said:

Mark, child, what I say, they will cut off my head, and perhaps make thee a king: but mark what I say, you must not be a king so long as your brothers Charles and James do live; for they will cut off your brothers' heads too (when they can catch them) and cut off thy head too, at last; and therefore I charge you, do not be made a king by them.

The little prince, who had listened to his father's words with great attentiveness, gave an answer worthy of one far beyond his years, when he uttered the reassuring words to his father:

I will be torn in pieces first.

The King put his son down and kissed him. He kissed his daughter too, gave them most of his remaining jewels to take away, then blessed them both. As the children were led away by Bishop Juxton, His Majesty retired to his bedchamber.

At about half past five the King woke and said to his servant, Thomas Herbert, 'I will get up, I have a great work to do this day.' The King again addressed his servant with the words, 'Herbert, this is my second marriage day; I would be as trim today as may be, for before to-night I hope to be espoused to my blessed Jesus.' Dressing and His Majesty's painstaking toilet lasted a full hour. The King's chestnut coloured hair and beard were flecked with grey. He had Herbert trim his beard with great precision. Realizing that it must be cold outside, for the fire in the hearth could not entirely dispel the chill that seeped into the chamber, the King chose the clothing he would wear with an eye to warmth. He told Herbert, 'I will not have the people see me shiver in the cold lest they think me afraid.' During his toiletry preparations the King also remarked 'I fear not death. Death is not terrible to me. I bless God I am prepared.' He put on two linen shirts, over which he dressed in a waistcoat of rich, red-striped silk, brocaded with silver and yellow. His doublet and breeches were of black satin. The King also wore a short black velvet cloak. He also wore earrings, each a pearl surmounted by a small gold crown; and also the blue ribbon, golden emblem and badge of the Order of the Garter.

The King gave some final instructions for the distribution of gifts and shortly after His Majesty's preparations were completed, William Juxton, Bishop of London arrived, to give him communion. The King spoke privately with Juxton for an hour, and then received the Sacrament. At first His Majesty thought that the Bishop had chosen the Gospel especially for the occasion, but was much impressed when Juxton informed him that it was the lesson ordained for the day in the Prayer Book, the twenty-seventh Chapter of St Matthew, the Passion of our Lord. This proved greatly significant to those Royalists who would later espouse Charles I's martyrdom.

Oliver Cromwell. Author's collection

A little while before ten o'clock, a man in the scarlet uniform of a colonel in the Puritan army knocked lightly on the door of the King's bedchamber. There was no reply, so he knocked again, this time more firmly. The door was opened by Herbert and the colonel was admitted. Visibly trembling, Colonel Hacker told the King that it was time to go to Whitehall. His Majesty replied that he would come 'presently' and after a few moments of prayer with the bishop, he took Juxton's hand saying, 'Come, let us go.' The King remarked to Hacker, 'I am grateful for a walk on such a cold morning. It will restore my circulation.' The party left St James's Palace by a door leading into the palace garden. Colonel Tomlinson was waiting for the King. The snow had stopped falling but the ground was hard and the sky looked threatening. As the party made its way through St James's Park to Whitehall, with his hat in his hand, Colonel Tomlinson walked on one side of the King, Bishop Juxton on the other, Thomas Herbert followed behind. This small group was quickly surrounded by the two companies of infantry, who were to provide the escort. When they reached the edge of St James's Park an open wooden staircase led into the adjoining buildings of Whitehall. From the staircase, the King passed along the gallery above the Tilt-yard, which was hung with many portraits from the Royal collection, then he crossed King Street by the upper floor of the Holbein Gate, then he was taken to the chamber in which until recently he had slept. There, at about half-past ten, he was left with Herbert and Juxton.

The Palace of Whitehall seen from the River Thames. The Banqueting House dominates the left background. Author's collection

At noon a servant appeared to enquire of His Majesty what he would like for dinner. The King had eaten nothing since the previous night, intending that no food should pass his lips excepting the Sacrament. When the King replied 'Nothing', Bishop Juxton urged the King to take something, with the words, 'But your Majesty, no one can tell how long you must wait. In this bitter cold you might faint when you go out there.' The King realizing the bishop's good sense, said, 'Perhaps a manchet and a glass of claret.' The King drank the wine and ate half the manchet (a small white loaf).

Herbert took Bishop Juxton aside, ashen faced and trembling, he said 'Your reverence, I cannot answer for my actions any longer. His Majesty ordered me to have this ready, but I shall not be able to endure the sight of what they will do to him.' Herbert then handed Juxton a white linen embroidered cap. As he took the cap, Juxton said, 'I will see to that. You can wait in the Banqueting Hall.' It was almost two o'clock in the afternoon when Colonel Hacker knocked on the King's door. Juxton and Herbert fell to their knees weeping. The King ordered Herbert to open the door, this being done His Majesty along with Herbert and Bishop Juxton, followed Hacker along the corridors of the palace, between two ranks of soldiers which lined the entire route shoulder to shoulder. People had crowded into the palace to get a sight of the King, some were

The remnants of the Palace of Whitehall, seen in this engraving of 1724, twenty-six years after much of the palace was destroyed by fire. The Banqueting House can be seen on the left. Author's collection

The Banqueting House, Whitehall, August 2005. The author

praying, others gave him their blessings as he passed by. They finally reached the Banqueting House and passed through the dimly lit hall. Outside, masses of soldiers several ranks deep, held back an immense multitude of people. People peered through every available window and many watched from the rooftops. First to come out of the window was Colonel Hacker and his guard of soldiers. Next came the King with a firm and steady step, accompanied by Bishop Juxton. Then out stepped two masked men with false hair and beards, they went immediately to the block and stood silently by it. Colonel Tomlinson was also on the scaffold and so were several short-hand writers with notebooks, ready to take down what was said.

The King looked disdainfully at the sight that beheld him, for not only was the block unusually low but several staples had been driven into the planking and cords and pulleys had been laid out nearby in case he resisted, in order that he might be tied down. No such indignities were necessary, as, when the time came, the King did not resist. As for the executioner, although many rumours were in circulation in the preceding days before the execution as to his identity, and for some time afterwards, there is little doubt that the man who wielded the axe that struck off the head of the King was Richard Brandon, the City's principal hangman. Brandon had succeeded his father, Gregory Brandon, in his office in about 1639 and was generally referred to as 'young Gregory'. He lived near the Tower of London, in Rosemary Lane. In the preceding years he had beheaded several high profile prisoners including the Earl of

Strafford and William Laud, Archbishop of Canterbury. Brandon was noted for his efficiency and he prided himself on his dexterity with the axe. He never needed to strike more than once. On the scaffold, both the executioner and his assistant wore masks, false hair and beards, in the hope that they would not be recognized.

As the King looked towards the axe and the block, which was no more than ten inches off the ground, he asked Colonel Hacker if no higher one could be provided. 'It can be no higher, Sir', came the reply. His Majesty was allowed to speak as he chose. Out of a pocket the King took a small piece of paper, about four inches square, on which he had made some notes, he unfolded it and began to speak. As his voice could not reach beyond the assembled troops he spoke to those gathered on the scaffold. The King began:

> *I shall be very little heard of anybody here* [meaning the wider audience of spectators], *I shall therefore speak a word unto you here,* [meaning those assembled about him on the scaffold]. *Indeed I could hold my peace very well, but I think it is my duty, to God first, and to my country, for to clear myself both as an honest man, a good King, and a good Christian ... I think it is not very needful for me to insist long upon this, for all the world knows that I never did begin a war first with the two Houses of Parliament ... God forbid I should lay it on the two Houses of Parliament ... I do believe that ill instruments between them and me have been the chief cause of all this bloodshed.*

He told the assembled company that if as a King, he denied the justice of the sentence against him he saw his fate as God's judgment on him. Having spoken these words the King then immediately made reference to the one great regret of his life, which had lain heavy on his conscience since May 1641. He had allowed his true and loyal friend and ally, Thomas Wentworth, Earl of Strafford, to go to the scaffold, when unscrupulous parliamentarians, unable to find him guilty of any crime, had resorted to using an Act of Parliament, the Act of Attainder, to find him guilty, and as one commentator at the time said, murdered him with the sword of justice. Although the King did not speak the name of Strafford, for most of those who heard or later read his words, no further explanation was necessary. The King simply uttered:

> *I will only say this, that an unjust sentence that I suffered to take effect is punished now by an unjust sentence upon me, that is, so far I have said, to show you that I am an innocent man.*

The King then said that he had forgiven all the world:

> *and even those in particular that have been the chief causers of my death: who they are, God knows, I do not desire to know, I pray God forgive them ... I wish that they may repent, for indeed they have committed a great sin in that particular; I pray God, with St Stephen, that this be not laid to their charge. Nay, not only so, but that they may take the right way to the peace of the Kingdom: for my charity commands me not only to forgive particular men, but my charity commands me to endeavour to the last gasp the peace of the Kingdom. So, Sirs, I do wish with all my soul, (and I do hope there is some here will carry it further) that they may endeavour the peace of the Kingdom ...*

Of his enemies in politics, the King went on to say:

> *... they would achieve nothing by unjust conquest; they must learn to know their duty to God, the King – "that is, my successors" – and the people. They should call a national council to settle the affairs of the Church. As for the King –*

At this point, the King broke off speaking as he noticed that one of the officers had accidentally touched the axe. The King said to him:

> *Hurt not the axe, that may hurt me.*

The King resumed his speech and having completed his passage about his political adversaries, he turned to the subject of the people and went on:

> *Truly I desire their liberty and freedom as much as anybody whomsoever; but I must tell you their liberty and freedom consists in having of government, those laws by which their life and their goods may be most their own. It is not for having a share in government, Sirs, that is nothing pertaining to them. A subject and a sovereign are clear different things ... Sirs, it was for this that now I am come here. If I would have given way to an arbitrary way, for to have all laws changed according to the power of the sword, I needed not have come here; and therefore I tell you (and I pray God it be not laid to your charge) that I am the Martyr of the people ...*

He added that he had so little time to put his thoughts in better order, then at the prompting of Bishop Juxton made reference to his religion and after stating that he had almost forgotten to vindicate himself and his Church from the accusation of Popery, stated:

> *... that I die a Christian according to the profession of the Church of England, as I found it left me by my father ... I have a good cause and I have a gracious God; I will say no more.*

The King then turned to the strangely disguised figures standing by the block. Perhaps because of the unusual circumstances or simply out of fear, the executioner did not ask the customary forgiveness of his victim. The King said that he would pray briefly, then sign for him to strike. He also asked how he should arrange his hair so as not to impede the axe. This being done, with the help of Juxton, he put on his embroidered linen cap and pushed his hair beneath it. Juxton spoke to the King:

> *There is one stage more, which though turbulent and troublesome, yet it is a very short one; you may consider it will soon carry you a very great way; it will carry you from Earth to Heaven; and there you shall find to your great joy, the prize you hasten to, a Crown of Glory.*

To this the King replied,

> *I go from a corruptible to an incorruptible crown, where no disturbance can be, no disturbance in the world.*

The King then removed his 'George', the insignia of the Garter and gave it to Juxton with one last word:

> *Remember.*

He took off his cloak and doublet, then donned his cloak again and stood for a few moments raising his hands and his eyes as if to heaven, then he removed his cloak once more, and before he submitted himself to the block, said to the executioner:

> *You must set it fast.*

The executioner replied:

It is fast, Sir.

The King then said:

It might have been a little higher.

The executioner assured His Majesty with the words:

It can be no higher, Sir.

Then the King lay down and placed his head on the block. His Majesty had now partially disappeared from view, to all but a few

The execution of Charles I outside the Banqueting House, Whitehall, 30 January 1649. The representation of the scaffold is inaccurate, as it extended to the left of the building and into the recessed portion, where a window had been removed through which the King and execution party stepped. Author's collection

onlookers, mostly those who had high vantage points, as the low block and profusion of black drapery obscured the view. The executioner stooped to make sure the King's hair was not in the way, and as he did so His Majesty clearly thought he was about to strike and called out:

Stay for the sign.

The executioner replied:

I will, an' it please Your Majesty.

A cloak of deathly silence had wrapped itself around Whitehall. Not a sound came from the troops or the crowd. Then, within a few seconds the King stretched out his hands to give the sign and immediately the executioner swung the axe through the still, cold air and the spectators saw the flash of the axe as the executioner brought it down and at one blow severed the King's head from his body. On the death of Charles I, so perished also the Divine Right of Kings.

One spectator wrote:

At the instant when the blow was given there was such a dismal, universal groan among the people as I never heard before and desire I may never hear again.

Bust of King Charles I, Banqueting House, Whitehall. The plaque below states that it was through a window above (now blocked up) that the King stepped onto the scaffold. The author

The executioner's assistant held the King's head high for all to see. But, contrary to erroneous reports, he did not pronounce the words he had been told to say: 'Behold the head of a traitor!' Some believe this was because he was afraid he would be recognized by his voice, I prefer to believe that his sympathies did not lie with the regicides.

The moment the King was dead, a troop of horse stationed at the north end of King Street and a troop stationed at the south end, advanced to disperse the crowd, who quickly disappeared up various side lanes and alleys. Some of the guards and spectators managed to dip handkerchiefs in the King's blood and others scraped up earth from beneath the scaffold. Meanwhile, the King's body was carried with great reverence from the scaffold and into the Banqueting House, where it was placed in a coffin before being conveyed under the watchful eyes of Herbert and Juxton, to a room within the palace where it was to be embalmed by the surgeon Mr Trapham and his assistant. After the body had been embalmed it was then placed in a coffin lined with lead, covered with a black velvet pall and removed to St James's Palace, where it remained for a week. It was the House of Commons who finally gave the order for the King's burial. They decided against Henry VII's Chapel in Westminster Abbey, where his father and mother had been buried. It was too close to home for comfort and they did not want Charles I's grave to become a place of pilgrimage. They settled upon St. George's Chapel, Windsor and put the Duke of Richmond in charge of the arrangements, which were to be at a cost of no more than five hundred pounds. The coffin was conveyed to Windsor Castle on 7 February. The following day, it was taken from the King's bedchamber to St George's Hall. At a little before three o'clock in the afternoon, the King's coffin was carried into St George's chapel. Snow was falling heavily and as the coffin was carried up the steps of the chapel, the black velvet pall was white over. Another sign, some said, of the King's martyrdom. The coffin of Charles I was placed in a vault beside that of Henry VIII, in a space originally intended for his sixth wife, and surviving widow, Katherine Parr, who remarried and was buried

Carnifex Maiestatis Regis Anglia

A fanciful depiction of General Fairfax holding the severed head of King Charles I. Author's collection

elsewhere. Jane Seymour, Henry's third wife, occupied the space on the opposite side of the vault.

It was recorded that executioner Richard Brandon, swore when the King was condemned to death that he would never raise a hand against him. Attempts at bribery and intimidation were unsuccessful. Then, on 30 January 1649, he was 'fetched out of bed by a troop of horse' and marched to the scaffold to do his duty. Brandon received £30 for his troubles and a pomander, a clove-studded orange, from the dead King's pocket. Within five months of the King's execution Brandon, his supposed executioner, was himself dead. Some say he died of a broken heart. Brandon died on 20 June 1649, his body buried the following day in St Mary's churchyard, Whitechapel. The entry in the church records was recorded as follows, 'Rich. Brandon, a man out of Rosemary Lane.' And in the margin in a different hand was added, 'This R Brandon is supposed to have cut off the head of Charles the First.'

The execution of Charles I was entirely unconstitutional. For it was an established principle that no man may be sentenced without

Contemporary propaganda depicting the 'Royall Oak of Brittayne'. To Royalists, Cromwell was the barbarian who destroyed the golden age by hacking down the royal tree. Author's collection

the lawful judgment 'of his peers', and no court of law may be established without the consent of the King, Lords and Commons; and the court which tried the King was established by the authority of the Rump (the surviving embodiment of the Parliamentary cause) alone, a mere caricature of a representative body. However, in this revolutionary period, one of a suspension of law, pending reconstruction and settlement on a new basis, old values were ignored and the law completely disregarded. The legal course would have been to depose the King, on the basis that he had broken his compact with the nation, sworn to at his coronation. Of Charles I, Sir Winston Churchill wrote:

Statue of Oliver Cromwell outside the Palace of Westminster. The author

He was not a martyr in the sense of one who dies for a spiritual ideal. His own kingly interests were mingled at every stage with the larger issues. Some have sought to represent him as the champion of the small or humble man against the rising money-power. This is fanciful. He cannot be claimed as the defender of English liberties, nor wholly of the English Church, but none the less he died for them, and by his death preserved them not only to his son and heir, but to our own day.

CHAPTER 4

Claude Duval, the Dashing Highwayman
1670

Here lies Duval: reader, if male thou art,
Look to thy purse: if female, to thy heart.

Other parts of London may lay claim to associations with one who might arguably be regarded as the most infamous highwayman England ever had, namely Dick Turpin, but the West End can certainly lay claim to the most dashing. One January night in 1670, Claude Duval (or Du Vall), that most glamorous of gentlemen of the road, as some would have it, more commonly known as highwaymen, was arrested at the *Hole-in-the-Wall* public house (now *The Marquis of Granby*), established in 1638, on the corner of Chandos Place and Bedfordbury, a narrow thoroughfare, running south to north and sandwiched between the Strand and New Row, Covent Garden. Unwisely Duval had ventured back to England from France, where he had taken refuge when things became too hot for him. There was still a price on his head, and when he reached London, brimming with over-confidence, he let his guard slip. Prone to heavy indulgence in wine, women and song, on the night of his arrest, he became outrageously drunk and completely incapacitated, which was fortunate for the bailiff and his men who arrested him, for as well as three pistols in his pocket, one of which could shoot twice, he had an 'excellent sword' by his side. One commentator wrote:

... which, managed by such a hand and heart, must without a doubt, have done wonders ... I have heard it attested by those that knew how

good a marksman he was, and his excellent way of fencing, that had he been sober, it was impossible he could have killed less than ten.

Born at Domfront in Normandy in 1643, the son of a miller, Claude Duval went to Rouen, when he was fourteen, and found work with a group of exiled English royalists. He came to England at the Restoration in the service of the third Duke of Richmond, as a footman, and he developed a good command of English. However, he did not remain a footman for long. Duval had developed a taste for fine clothes and high living. Following daring robberies in Highgate, Islington and Holloway, and one exploit which led to a road being named Duval Lane, Hampstead (now Platt's Lane), his name soon became synonymous with highway robbery. He sometimes worked with a gang but many of his legendary exploits seem to have occurred largely when he was working alone. Regarded as a true knight of the road, he was certainly the most charming, to both male and female victims, he dressed fashionably, sometimes flamboyantly, was courteous in both speech and manner and it was said that his Gallic flourish made him particularly attractive to the ladies. Despite his charms, like many other more ruthless highwaymen, Duval was not averse to relieving his victims of large sums of money, jewels and trinkets, whenever the opportunity presented itself, although he conducted the proceedings in his own inimitable way, which endeared him to some of his victims, at least. Duval was also a highly dexterous card-sharp and won considerable sums by 'slipping a card'. It was said of him at gaming he was so

A seventeenth-century game of cards. Author's collection

expert that few men in his age were able to play with him. No man living could slip a card more dexterously than he, nor better understood the advantages that could be taken of an adversary; yet to appearance, no man played fairer.

In 1666 a newsletter carried the following report:

Last Monday week in Holborn Fields, while several gentlemen were traveling to Newmarket, to the races there, a Highwayman very politely begged their purses, for he said he was advised that he should win a great sum if he adventured some guineas with the competers at Newmarket on a certain horse called "Boopeepe", which my Lord Excetter [Exeter] was to run a match. He was so pressing that they resigned their money to his keeping (not without sight of his pistols); he telling them that, if he would give him their names and the names of the places where they might be found, he would return to them that [they] had lent, at usary [with interest]. It is thought that his venture was not favourable, for the gentlemen have not received neither principle or interest. It is thought that it was Monsieur Claud [sic] Du Vall, or one of his knot, that ventured the gentlemen's money for them.

The Marquis of Granby, *formerly the* Hole in the Wall, *established in 1638, situated at the corner of Bedfordbury and Chandos Place, where Claude Duval was apprehended in January 1670.* The author

One time Duval met with Esquire Roper, master of the buck-hounds to King Charles II, as he was hunting in Windsor Forest. Duval came across Roper in a thicket and took advantage of the cover. He commanded him to stand and deliver his money, or else he would shoot him. Mr Roper, to save his life, gave Duval a purse containing at least fifty guineas. Duval afterwards bound him neck and heels, fastened his horse by him, and rode away. When the squire was unbound he hastened to Windsor, and as he entered the town was met by Sir Stephen Fox who asked him whether or not he had had any sport. The squire replied, with great passion:

> *Yes, sir, I have had sport enough from a son of a whore, who made me pay damned dear for it. He bound me neck and heels, contrary to my desire, and then took fifty guineas from me, to pay him for his labour, which I had much rather he had omitted.*

Claude Duval holds up Squire Roper, the King's master of buck-hounds, in a thicket in Windsor Forest and relieves him of his heavy purse. Author's collection

In 1668 Duval's name headed a list of highwaymen mentioned in a Royal Proclamation, which offered £20 for his capture. Duval's charming manners and good looks are reputed to have given him many amorous conquests, ranging from serving girls to respectable widows, sometimes whores and often ladies of high rank. Following his arrest he was taken to Newgate, tried, convicted and sentenced to death. During his incarceration in Newgate, he was visited by many noble ladies. Despite their pleas for clemency, at the express command of the King, Duval was not pardoned.

Claude Duval was twenty-seven-years-old when he was executed at Tyburn on Friday 21 January 1670 and was accompanied to the scaffold by many ladies of high rank, who wore masks to disguise their identities. In *Tyburn Tree Its History and Annals,* a work which draws on many old documents, Alfred Marks records:

After he had hanged a convenient time, he was cut down, and, by persons well dressed, carried into a mourning-coach, and so conveyed to the Tangier-tavern in St. Giles, where he lay in state all that night, the room hung with black cloth, the hearse covered with escutcheons, eight wax-tapers burning, and as many tall gentlemen with long black cloakes [sic] *attending; mum was the word, great silence expected from all that visited, for fear of disturbing this sleeping lion. And this ceremony had lasted much longer, had not one of the judges (whose name I must not mention here, lest he should incur the displeasure of the ladies) sent to disturb the pageantry.*

Dr William Pope, who wrote the biography *Memoirs of Monsieur Du Vall*, in 1670 (from which most of what has since been written about Duval seems to

King Charles II, who expressly forbade Duval's reprieve from the gallows. Author's collection

derive), claimed that Duval left behind a 'dying confession' that he had intended to read at Tyburn, but changed his mind. However, in the *Complete Newgate Calender Volume 1,* it states:

A seventeenth-century execution at Tyburn. Author's collection

As they were undressing him, in order to his lying-in-state, one of his friends put his hand into his pocket and found therein the following paper, which as appears by the contents, he intended as a legacy to the ladies. It was written in a very fair hand:-

"I should be very ungrateful to you, fair English ladies, should I not acknowledge the obligations you have laid me under. I could not have hoped that a person of my birth, nation, education and condition could have had charms enough to captivate you all; though the contrary has appeared, by your firm attachment to my interest, which you have not abandoned even in my last distress. You have visited me in prison, and even accompanied me to an ignominious death.

From my experience of your former loves, I am confident that many among you would be glad to receive me to your arms, even from the gallows.

How mightily and how generously have you rewarded my former services! Shall I ever forget the universal consternation that appeared upon your faces when I was taken; your chargeable visits to me in Newgate; your shrieks and swoonings when I was condemned, and your zealous intercession and importunity for my pardon! You could not have erected fairer pillars of honour and respect to me had I been Hercules, able to get fifty of you with child in one night.

It has been the misfortune of several English gentlemen to die at this place, in the time of the late usurpation, upon the most honourable occasion that ever presented itself; yet none of these, as I could ever learn, received so many marks of your esteem as myself. How much the greater, therefore is my obligation.

It does not, however, grieve me that your intercession for me proved ineffectual; for now I shall die with a healthful body, and, I hope, a prepared mind. My confessor has shown me the evil of my ways, and wrought in me a true repentance. Whereas, had you prevailed for my

Duval Court, 36 Bedfordbury, built opposite where Claude Duval was apprehended. The author

*life, I must in gratitude have devoted it to your service, which would
certainly have made it very short; for had you been sound, I should have
died of a consumption; if otherwise, of a pox.*

Duval was given a fine funeral at St Paul's Church, Covent Garden
and according to popular legend, was buried in the chancel and a
white marble stone laid over the site of his tomb. It bore his family's
arms, under which was engraved this epitaph:

Here lies Duval: reader, if male thou art,
Look to thy purse: if female, to thy heart.
Much havoc hath he made of both: for all
Men he made stand, and women he made fall.
The Second Conqueror of the Norman race,
Knights to his arms did yield, and ladies to his face.
Old Tyburn's glory, England's bravest thief:
Duval, the ladies' joy: Duval, the ladies' grief.

Like other monuments to those who were buried within St Paul's
Church, Covent Garden during the seventeenth and most of the
eighteenth century, that of Claude Duval was probably destroyed in
the fire that wreaked havoc in the church in 1795, or perhaps,
because it was supposedly in the chancel, it has been tiled over
during renovations and repairs. I have read one account that
intimates Duval's body was exhumed and possibly taken to France
for reburial. This assertion, as far as I have been able to ascertain is
unsubstantiated and whether it is based on fact or is simply yet
another fanciful story within the intricate web of legends associated
with this enigmatic highwayman, I have been unable to establish. To
this day there is still a reminder of Duval, very close to where he was
arrested and quite close to the church where, as far as most people
with a passing interest are concerned, believe he still lies buried. At
36 Bedfordbury stands a block of flats named Duval Court.

CHAPTER 5

The Burning of Catherine Hayes
1726

... instead of the expected splash there was a thud, as the water was shallow and the head and bucket had landed in mud.

Catherine Hayes was born Catherine Hall of poor parents, in Birmingham in 1690. In 1705, when Catherine was fifteen, she met some army officers, who took to the attractive young girl and persuaded her to join them in their quarters. Never one for letting an opportunity pass by her, Catherine took them at their word, and, for a while, became their collective mistress, until they moved on. From being little more than a kept whore, Catherine became maid to a Warwickshire Farmer, named Hayes. The farmer had a son named John, who was a carpenter. He fell in love with his father's attractive, young maid and before long, twenty-one-year-old John Hayes had stolen away to Worcester and secretly married Miss Catherine Hall. Once Catherine had hooked her man, her true nature began to surface, she became argumentative and most disagreeable to her in-laws. After six years of marriage, she was growing bored with life in the country and she persuaded her husband to move to London.

John Hayes came of an industrious family and he adopted their principles. In London he thrived in business, becoming a successful coal-merchant, pawnbroker and moneylender. He traded from premises in Tyburn Road (today's Oxford Street). In a little over ten years, he had made enough money to enable him to sell his shop and take lodgings nearby.

This evil, scheming harridan of a wife made her industrious husband's life miserable and once boasted to neighbours that she would think it no more sin to murder him than to kill a dog. She said that her husband was miserly

Catherine Hayes. Author's collection

and mean, which if it were true, was at odds with her own desire for luxury.

At the beginning of 1725 a young man named Thomas Billings called at the Hayes's lodgings. He was a tailor by trade and Catherine told her husband he was an old friend and John Hayes allowed Billings to stay with them. When John Hayes ventured out of London on business, his wife took Billings into her bed. While the husband was away, the lovers took advantage of his absence by throwing parties and being frivolous with money. When John Hayes returned, he gave his wife a beating. Billings remained in residence apparently blameless of any indiscretions in the eyes of his unsuspecting host.

Not long after John Hayes returned to London, another young 'friend' of Catherine's turned up on the doorstep. His name was Thomas Wood. Wood also shared Catherine's favours whenever the opportunity allowed. She cajoled Wood into believing that her husband was an evil man and by offering him a share in her husband's estate, should she become a widow, which amounted to the then very large sum of fifteen hundred pounds, persuaded him to agree to help her kill him. Catherine had at the very least a fertile imagination. She told Wood that her husband was an atheist and that he had killed their two children and buried them under fruit trees. It was not long before an opportunity to dispose of John Hayes presented itself.

After being out of London for a little while, Thomas Wood returned on 1 March 1725. When he called at the Hayes's lodgings, he found John and Catherine Hayes in high spirits with Thomas Billings, indulging in a drinking session. Wood joined in with the party and a challenge was issued by the boastful Mr Wood that he could consume more wine than Hayes and still remain sober. He had already consumed six bottles. Wood said if he won the bet then Hayes should pay for the wine. Hayes agreed. Leaving Hayes at these lodgings, Catherine, Billings and Wood went to the *Brawn's Head* in Bond Street, where they drank a pint of 'best mountain wine' between them, and a further six pints were taken back to their lodgings. While his wife, Billings and Wood drank beer, Hayes downed the six bottles of wine, apparently with little difficulty. However, Catherine had sent out for more wine and as Hayes drank his seventh bottle, he collapsed on the floor. A few minutes passed before he came round and staggered into the adjacent bedroom. Shortly afterwards Billings went into the room and finding Hayes face down on the bed, dealt him a violent blow with a coal hatchet (one of the tools used during Hayes's time as a coal merchant.

atherine Hayes, Thomas Billings and homas Wood, dismembering the body of e murdered John Hayes. Author's collection

Several such hatchets were found in the house), which fractured his skull, as Hayes stirred he was dealt two more blows which finished him off. The noise of the blows, delivered with such violence that they could be heard on the floor above, brought a neighbour down to investigate. Mrs Springate, who lived in lodgings above those of the Hayes's, came downstairs to complain about the noise. Catherine Hayes apologized and told her that her husband had invited some guests, who would be leaving shortly. Mrs Springate having returned to her own quarters, it was now necessary to dispose of the body as quickly and as quietly as possible.

Notwithstanding the butchery that followed, the bedding was already drenched and the walls and ceiling of the bedchamber spattered with blood. Catherine apparently remained cool and calm. She suggested that in order to avoid identification, her husband's head should be cut off and disposed of separately. This, her accomplices agreed to do. They resorted to sawing through the neck with a knife, as the sound of chopping at so late an hour might bring Mrs Springate upon them again. The head was placed over a bucket to catch the blood, while the neck was sawn through. The two men balked at the idea of Catherine's to boil the head to remove the flesh. Despite their precautions to keep the noise to a minimum, Mrs Springate found herself, once again, obliged to call downstairs. She later said in evidence that Catherine told her that her husband had been called away suddenly and was getting ready to leave. While preparations were being made to dispose of the blood, which was poured down various sinks, Catherine put on a convincing performance calling out goodbye to her husband, in the hope she would be heard by the neighbours, which of course, she was.

Wood and Billings took the severed head out of the house in a bucket concealed beneath Billings's coat, while Catherine attempted to wash the bloodstains from the unvarnished floorboards. Despite washing them and scraping them with a knife, the stains were still visible. At risk of being stopped by the watch at so late an hour, as it was well after midnight, Billings and Wood made their way to Whitehall and arrived at the River Thames, where they discovered to their dismay that the tide was out. They dare not wade across the foreshore for fear of attracting attention, so they walked on past Westminster to Horseferry wharf (where the present Horseferry Road meets Lambeth Bridge). There they went to the end of the dock and threw the head in the river and the bucket after it. However, instead of the expected splash there was a thud, as the water was shallow and the head and bucket had landed in mud. A night watchman heard the sound as the head and bucket hit the river bed, and a lighterman on board a boat saw the bucket being thrown into the river, but as the night was dark it was only at daybreak that night watchman Robinson, saw the bucket and head floating near the shore, from where they were retrieved. Meanwhile, Billings and Wood had made their way back to Catherine, expecting the head to have floated away on the next tide. They discussed how to dispose of the body. Catherine had procured a wooden box but it was not large enough to take the body. They cut off the arms, then the legs at the knees but it still proved too large to fit in the box. They then hacked off the legs at the thighs and somehow managed to fit all the pieces into the box, which at nine o'clock that night they took out of the house wrapped in a blanket. They went north to Marylebone, where they took the remains of John Hayes's body out of the box and put them in a blanket and threw the package into a pond, where it sunk.

Meanwhile the severed head had been handed over to parish officers. It was washed to remove the blood and mud from the face and hair and the hair was combed. It was then attached to a pole and placed in the churchyard of St Margaret's Westminster, adjacent to Westminster

Abbey, for several days, in the hope that someone would recognize it. Eventually, an organ-builder named Bennet came forward to say the head resembled an acquaintance of his named John Hayes and a journeyman-tailor named Mr Patrick also recognized it. Patrick went to the *Dog and Dial* in Monmouth Street, where John and Catherine Hayes used to drink. Billings happened to be there and when it was pointed out to Patrick that he was the Hayes's lodger, Billings said he had left Hayes in bed that morning.

John Hayes's head exhibited outside St Margaret's Church, Westminster, in an attempt to identify it. Author's collection

During the next few days, when enquiries were made of Catherine as to the whereabouts of her husband, her inventive mind came up with the ridiculous story that he had killed a man and absconded. On being asked if the head was her husband's victim, she replied that the body had been buried entire. On being questioned by different visitors to her lodgings, she told a different story to each. It was not long before suspicion fell on her. She moved lodgings and took Billings, Wood and Mrs Springate with her; and began collecting her husband's debts. By this time the severed head was beginning to decompose, so it was placed in a jar of spirits to preserve it.

The body parts were found in the pond in Marylebone and as Catherine received more and more visitors enquiring after her husband, the net closed in. As it had been established that Billings and Wood were with Hayes the last time he was seen alive, when a warrant was issued for the arrest of the murderers, their names were included on it. Catherine Hayes was arrested by Mr Justice Lambert in person, assisted by two officers of the Life Guards. Billings was taken at the same time, as he was in her bedchamber. Mr Justice Lambert asked Billings if he had been sleeping with Mrs Hayes, Billings said no, he was mending his stockings. The magistrate pointed out that he must have been doing it in the dark as there was neither fire nor candle. Mrs Springate was also arrested but was later released.

When Catherine asked if she could see the head that had been displayed in St Margaret's churchyard, Mr Justice Lambert went with her to the barber-surgeon, Mr Westbrook, who was looking after it. When Catherine was shown the head, she took the glass in which the head was preserved and called out:

It is my dear husband's head.

Catherine's performance knew no bounds. She shed tears as she embraced the container and the head having been lifted out of the spirit, she kissed it rapturously and begged to be given a lock of its hair. As the barber-surgeon remarked that she had already had enough of her husband's blood, Catherine swooned away.

Wood was arrested and on hearing that the body had been found in the pond, confessed his part in the crime. Catherine obstinately refused to admit her guilt. She was an object of curiosity in Newgate, where she told varying accounts of events to the many visitors she received. Eventually she admitted that she had wanted to get rid of her husband and had persuaded Billings and Wood to help her. At the trial she pleaded to be exempted from the penalty of petty treason on the grounds that she had not struck the fatal blow herself. However, her plea was disregarded and she was told the law must take its course. Thomas Billings and Thomas Wood were condemned to death by hanging and afterwards to be hung in chains. Catherine sent messages to her two lovers regretting that she had involved them. When she saw Billings in chapel she held his hand and showed other signs of affection.

However, Wood was ailing fast in Newgate. He cheated the hangman and died of a fever, on 4 May, in the condemned cell.

On 9 May 1726 Thomas Billings was hanged at Tyburn and later his body was suspended in chains a little over a hundred yards from the gallows and not far from the pond where John Hayes's body had been disposed of. When the executioner, Richard Arnet, came to fetch Catherine, she asked him if he had killed her 'dear child' yet. This prompted speculation that he was Catherine's son by a previous connection. Although the ages of Wood and Billings were not recorded, they were believed to have both been teenagers.

At Tyburn, when Catherine had finished her devotions, in pursuance of her sentence an iron chain was put round her body, with which she was fixed to a stake near the gallows. Faggots were then placed around her and the executioner lit the fire. On these occasions, when women were burned for petty treason, it was customary to strangle them, by means of a rope round the neck and pulled by the executioner, so they were dead before the flames

reached the body. But Catherine was literally burned alive, as Arnet let go of the rope sooner than usual, in consequence of the flames reaching his hands. The fire burned fiercely round her, and the spectators watched her pushing away the faggots, while she 'rent the air with her cries and lamentations.' Other faggots were instantly thrown on her; but she survived amidst the flames for a considerable time, and her body was not perfectly reduced to ashes until three hours later.

The burning of Catherine Hayes at Tyburn, 9 May 1726. Author's collection

Chapter 6

Murdered by a Poet
1727

I am a dead man, and was stabbed cowardly.

In December 1727, Richard Savage (1697–1743) English poet and satirist and intimate friend of Dr Samuel Johnson, found himself on trial for his life, charged with murder, following a quarrel in a West End coffee-house. Savage was the illegitimate son of the Countess of Macclesfield, the result of a love affair with Captain Richard Savage, afterwards Earl Rivers. He was born on or about 10 January 1697. The young Savage grew up having been shoved from pillar to post, being placed in the care of a series of families, but despite his unconventional upbringing, his literary talents emerged. At the age of eight he had been placed at the grammar school in St Albans. When Savage was fifteen he came across some papers which explained the mystery of his birth and the contrivances that had been carried on to conceal his true origin. Lady Macclesfield had secured a divorce from her husband and married Lord Rivers. As their son grew up, his mother nurtured a deep hatred for him and many years later, only consented to settle an annuity of £50 on him after he had threatened to expose his parentage in his first volume of poems. Lord Rivers had died from an 'ulcer in the guts' at Bath in 1712.

On the evening of Monday 20 November 1727, Savage was in the company of two friends, William Merchant and James Gregory. All three men were the worse for drink when they entered Robinson's Coffee House, near Charing Cross. They forced their way into a room where a private party was just splitting up and began to quarrel with the departing guests. Merchant entered first and kicked over a table, whereupon angry words were exchanged and Savage and Gregory drew their swords. Savage was subject to fits of blind rage, particularly when drunk and on this occasion it seems he lost his head altogether. Mr Nuttal asked them to put them up, but they refused to do so. In the ensuing fight, Savage came up against James Sinclair, made several thrusts at his opponent and ran him through the belly. Sinclair fell, calling out as he did so:

I am a dead man, and was stabbed cowardly.

Someone put out the candles and in the darkness one of the maids received a cut to the head while trying to prevent Savage and Merchant fleeing the building. They did manage to escape but were quickly apprehended in a dark court nearby. Gregory was held in the coffee-house, where he was arrested. James Sinclair died the next morning but not before identifying Savage as his assailant. The deceased was attended by a clergyman and Sinclair told him he had been stabbed before he had time to draw his sword. Savage later said he had drawn his sword in self-defence. Savage, Merchant and Gregory were taken by soldiers and lodged in the roundhouse, and in the morning were carried before a magistrate who committed them to the Gatehouse, but following the death of James Sinclair, they were sent to Newgate. Arraigned before Sir Francis Page, notorious for his severity and commonly known as the 'hanging judge', their trial took place on Thursday 7 December, in the Old Bailey and lasted eight

Newgate Gaol, where Richard Savage, James Gregory and William Merchant were imprisoned. Author's collection

hours. In his summing-up, the judge instructed the jury that if the prisoners had acted without provocation, they were all three guilty of murder. He rejected the plea of hot blood and dismissed the character witness's evidence as irrelevant.

In his summing up Sir Francis Page said:

> *Gentlemen of the jury, you are to consider that Mr. Savage is a very great man, a much greater man than you or I, gentlemen of the jury; that he wears very fine clothes, much finer clothes than you or I, gentlemen of the jury; that he has abundance of money in his pocket, much more money than you or I, gentlemen of the jury; but, gentlemen of the jury, is it not a very hard case, gentlemen of the jury, that Mr. Savage should therefore kill you or me, gentlemen of the jury?*

The jury found Savage and Gregory guilty of murder, and Merchant, who had been unarmed, guilty of manslaughter. When Savage and Gregory were brought into court for sentencing, Savage, on being given an opportunity to address the court made a plea for clemency:

> *It is now, my Lord, too late to offer any thing by way of defence or vindication, nor can we expect from your Lordships, in this court, but the sentence which the law requires you, as judges to pronounce against men of our calamitous condition. – But we are also persuaded that as mere men, and out of this seat of rigorous justice, you are susceptive of the tender passions, and too humane, not to commiserate the unhappy situation of those whom the law sometimes perhaps – exacts from you to pronounce upon. No doubt you distinguish between offences which arise out of premeditation and a disposition habituated to vice or immorality and transgressions, which are the happy and unforeseen effects of [a] casual absence of reason, and sudden impulse of passion; we therefore hope you will contribute all you can to an extension of that mercy, which the gentlemen of the jury have been pleased to shew. Mr. Merchant, who (allowing facts as sworn against us by the evidence) has led us into this our calamity. I hope this will not be construed as if we meant to reflect upon that gentleman, or remove any thing from us upon him, or that we repine the more at our fate, because he has no participation of it. No, my Lord! For my part, I declare nothing could more soften my grief than to be without any companion in so great a misfortune.*

Savage's plea did nothing to soften the sentence as both he and Gregory were sentenced to die.

In Newgate, as Savage awaited his execution, loaded with chains weighing fifty pounds, he wrote two letters, one to his mother, begging her to visit him, the other to his friend, the actor Robert Wilks, oddly enough one of Savage's mother's many 'admirers'. His letter to Wilks ended:

> ... *As to death, I am easy and dare meet it like a man. All that touches me is the concern of my friends and a reconciliation with my mother. I cannot express the agony I felt when I wrote that letter to her. If you can find any decent excuse for showing it to Mrs Oldfield* [Anne Oldfield 1683–1730, the celebrated actress, who had rendered financial help to Savage, partly because of her admiration for him and partly because he had been left nothing in his father's will, whereas Savage's father, Earl Rivers, an admirer, had left her £500], *do, for I would have my friends and that admirable lady in particular, be satisfied I have done my duty ...*

Far from showing any kind of sympathy towards her son, the former Countess Rivers, now Mrs Brett, seemed to see her son's plight as a means of getting rid of him once and for all. She even went so far as to protest against mercy being shown. Fortunately for Savage, Mrs Oldfield was made of sterner stuff. Her many admirers at Court and in the higher echelons of society meant that many doors were open to her. She secured an interview with Sir Robert Walpole, First Lord of the Treasury. She spoke of Savage's many attributes, his talent, his unfair trial, the lack of premeditation and at the end of the interview, Sir Robert promised to do his best. Mrs Oldfield secured the help of Lady Hertford, patroness of literature, who used her influence also. Savage was released with a free pardon, after he had already ordered a suit of clothes for the scaffold. The pardon for both Savage and Gregory was ordered on 6 January 1728 and both were released on bail on 20 January. The pardon passed the seals on 1 February, thereafter Savage and Gregory could not plead His Majesty's pardon in court until the last day of the following sessions during the first week in March, when their bail was discharged. William Merchant, although convicted of manslaughter, claimed benefit of clergy and got off with a branding in the thumb.

CHAPTER 7

Killed in a Tiff Over a Wig
1735

... it entered the right eye of his opponent, penetrated the brain, and caused his death the next day.

T he Irish-born actor Charles Macklin (whose real name was M'Laughlin), was descended from Terence M'Laughlin, a landowner of County Down, whose son, William, married the daughter of John O'Flanagan, who owned large estates in Westmeath. The M'Laughlins considered themselves to be descendents of the ancient kings of Ireland. William M'Laughlin commanded a troop of horse in the army of James II, and was greatly distinguished for his valour, loyalty and zeal. He had one daughter, Mary, and one son, Charles. One of Charles Macklin's biographers, James Thomas Kirkman, wrote in 1779 that Macklin was born two months before the Battle of the Boyne, which took place on 1 July 1690.

In 1716 he joined a company of strolling players. Four years later he appeared in Bath and was engaged by Christopher Rich for the Lincoln's Inn Theatre. He was known as the Wild Irishman, noted for his joviality and excellent boxing skills. In 1732 he was engaged at Drury Lane, where he played secondary comic parts. Before he rose to greater heights, this hot blooded and intemperate actor in May 1735 quarrelled with his fellow actor Thomas Hallam over a wig, in the scene-room at Drury Lane, where the actors used to warm themselves and this resulted in Hallam's death. Macklin was fortunate not have been hanged for murder. Frances Asprey Congreve describes the event:

Mr Macklin had not long been settled as an actor at Drury-Lane, when an incident occurred which had nearly been attended with fatal consequences to him, and which certainly impressed an unfavourable opinion of him in the minds of the public during the rest of his days. On the 10th of May, 1735, a new farce was to be performed, called Trick for Trick, *written by Mr. Fabian, in which Mr. Macklin and Mr. Hallam both performed. In attiring for their respective characters, the*

The Piazza, Covent Garden. St Paul's Church dominates the centre background. Author's collection

latter gentleman had got possession of a wig belonging to the house, and which Mr. Macklin having performed in the preceding evening, he demanded the restoration of; with the demand, Hallam did not readily comply, and much foul language was exchanged by both parties. At length, Macklin, irritated at Hallam's non-compliance, and inflamed by the scurrility which passed between them, drove at him with a stick which he had in his hand, without any aim it is supposed, but unhappily with too fatal effect, as it entered the right eye of his opponent, penetrated the brain, and caused his death the next day.

Further notes from F A Congreve's account state that following the tragic event:

Mr. Macklin immediately absconded, and did not take his trial until the 12th of December, when he surrendered himself at the Old Bailey, where he was found guilty of manslaughter. It appeared by the evidence to be the result of a hasty fit of passion, unpremeditated and repented as soon as done. On this occasion, Mr. Rich, Mr. Fleetwood, Mr. Quin, Mr. Ryan, Mr. Thomson, Mr. Mills, and several others, appeared as candidates for his character, and testified him to be a man of quiet and peaceable disposition. It was not, however, until the 31ˢᵗ January, 1736, that he returned to his station at the theatre, by the performance of Ramillie, in Fielding's Miser.

At his trial at the Old Bailey, many of the most renowned actors of the day showed their support for their fellow player. He got off lightly, with a manslaughter verdict and was sentenced to be burned in the hand. Fortunately for himself, following this tragedy, Macklin's career went from strength to strength. On 14 February 1741, he made his first appearance as Shylock in *The Merchant of Venice* and became famous overnight by re-establishing the character as a dignified and tragic role instead of playing it as a comic role, to which the character had been assigned since the Restoration. He also played the characters of Iago and Macbeth to great acclaim.

Macklin lived a very long life and continued to work as an actor into extreme old age. However, as Macklin's career extended over such a long period, his associates and family seem to have credited him with ten more years, referring to him for the last seven years of his life as a centenarian. There is conflicting evidence as to his actual age at death, as the plate on his coffin and the memorial erected by his wife in St Paul's, Covent Garden, both give different ages.

Frances Asprey Congreve writes:

Theatre Royal Drury Lane. The frontage of the theatre was designed by Robert and James Adam in 1775 and built on Wren's earlier theatre. Author's collection

> *Mr. Macklin's last attempt upon the Stage was on the seventh of May, 1789, in the character of Shylock, for his own benefit. He made repeated efforts to overcome the stupor which clouded his reason, but in vain; after the performance of the first act, he was obliged to solicit the company to permit Mr. Ryder to finifh his part; this was immediately assented to, and the Father of British Drama took his farewell of the Stage, amid the thundering plaudits of his admirers.*

Congreve adds:

> *The remainder of his life cannot be viewed but with pity and concern. Though his mental faculties were so much impaired that he could not trace the features of his most intimate friends, and his sense of hearing so*

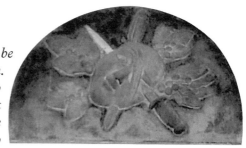

blunted that he could scarce catch at the words which were spoken to him, in a state little better than Swift's Struldbruggs, he continued to frequent the Theatre every night, he sat a miserable spectacle unable to receive entertainment, and apparently unconscious of what was passing in the house. He continued this practice until; a very short time to his death, which happened on Tuesday the 11th of July, 1797, at his lodgings in Tavistock-Row, at the advanced period of 97 years of age.

His remains were conveyed on the Saturday following, at half past one in the afternoon, to Covent Garden Church, the cavalcade consisted of a hearse and four, and three coaches and four ...

The corpse was taken into the vestry, and prayers were read over it in a very impressive manner, by the Rev. Mr. Ambrose, who had been a pupil of Mr. Macklin, and from the respect he bore his tutor, had come from Cambridge, to perform the last act of kindness, in reading over him the funeral service. – After the ceremony, the body was interred in the vault close to the north gate of the Church-yard, at the entrance to Covent-garden.

On the coffin plate was inscribed:

MR. CHARLES MACKLIN,
Comedian,
Died the 11th of July, 1797,
Aged 97 Years.

It was at Macklin's own request that he was interred in this particular vault, as he had a brother buried there. The expense of opening the vault was defrayed by Mr Harris, the liberal manager of Covent Garden Theatre. There was a rumour that the plate on Macklin's coffin had been altered before the vault was sealed to read 107 years. However, this was proved to be false, when during repairs and refurbishment to the churchyard during Victoria's reign, the vault was opened and it was found that the details on Macklin's coffin were as recorded and no alteration to the plate had been made.

The memorial stone to Charles Macklin on the south wall in St Paul's Church, Covent Garden. The author

CHAPTER 8

Shot by an Amorous Clergyman
1779

... Hackman discharged the pistol in his right hand first, and immediately afterwards discharged the pistol in his left hand at himself. Miss Reay was shot through the head. She, upon lifting her hand to her face, fell and died on the spot; but finding himself alive after he had shot at himself, and fallen also with his feet close to those of Miss Ray, Hackman beat his head with the pistol and called out, Kill me! Kill me!

One of London's most famous meeting places, the piazza of Covent Garden, was the scene of arguably the most notorious West End murder in the last quarter of the eighteenth century. It was also notable for the swiftness of justice which followed the tragic event. Martha Reay (or Ray), mistress of the Earl of Sandwich, was shot by the Reverend James Hackman, as she left the theatre on 7 April 1779.

Miss Martha Reay was born at Leicester Fields, Hertfordshire in 1742, the daughter of a stay maker, and at the age of fourteen was placed as an apprentice with Mrs Silver, of George's Court, St John's Lane, Clerkenwell, to be instructed in the business of a mantua-maker (maker of gowns). Attractive and highly accomplished, with a pleasant singing voice, Martha, in 1761, at the age of nineteen, caught the eye of the Earl of Sandwich (John Montagu, 4th Earl 1718–92, First Lord of the Admiralty), who took her as his mistress. Lord Sandwich had married in 1741 and his wife had borne him five children. Unfortunately, Lady Sandwich's state of mental health had declined since the birth of their fifth child in 1751 and in 1755 the couple had parted forever. Lady Sandwich was granted an apartment in Windsor Castle in which she lived with her unmarried sister, which enabled her to see her sons who were at school nearby at Eton. Her condition gradually declined until she was eventually formally declared insane by the Court of Chancery and made a ward of court. To a certain extent, as far as propriety allowed, among tolerant friends, Martha and Lord Sandwich lived together as man and wife. In the eighteenth century divorce was only possible by private Act of Parliament, which would have been a costly affair, and Sandwich's finances were always in a precarious state; and in view of Lady Sandwich's condition, divorce would not have been viewed favourably by both society and the general public. Instead Lord Sandwich made the best of the situation and settled down to life with Martha, it being the nearest he could manage to the happy marriage that had been lost to him forever. Martha and her children were referred to as Lord Sandwich's 'London family' and there was peace and harmony within the household. However, relations between his eldest surviving son and heir, Viscount Hinchbrook, were always strained. He resented his father's 'London family' and his father was determined to keep them apart.

There was to be a blight on this happy relationship between Martha Reay and Lord Sandwich. It came in the form of a young man named James Hackman. Hackman was born in Gosport, Hampshire of very respectable parents, who at the age of nineteen purchased him a commission in the 68th Regiment of Foot. Soon after he obtained his commission he was quartered at Huntingdon, where he was in charge of a recruiting party. He was invited by Lord Sandwich to his nearby country seat, Hinchbroke, to partake of the pleasures with his Lordship's other visitors that were provided in abundance. Horace Walpole said of Hinchbroke:

> ... *a very commodious, decent, irregular old House, much of it built in the time of Queen Elizabeth ... not an ugly spot for Huntingdonshire.*

It was at Hinchbroke that the youthful Hackman first met Martha Reay, who was under Lord Sandwich's protection. Hackman fell desperately in love with Miss Reay, and she, flattered by the young man's attentions, did little to discourage his advances. They exchanged letters for

Martha Reay. Author's collection

four years. These letters, purporting to be love letters between them were published shortly after Martha Reay's death, apparently with 'additions' made by the editor. Having failed to gain promotion in the army, perhaps because he believed it would improve his chances with Miss Reay, Hackman took holy orders and was appointed to a parish in Norfolk in 1768. When in London, Hackman would often attend the theatre and concerts with Martha and Lord Sandwich and the relationship between Martha and the amorous clergyman grew stronger. In fact, unbeknown to his Lordhip, the relationship reached such a peak of passion, that at its height, Martha was considering leaving Lord Sandwich and going to live with Hackman, and Hackman had every intention of marrying her. However, considering the circumstances of Martha Reay's position in life, the mistress of a peer of the realm, with five illegitimate children, I doubt if Hackman, a clergyman, could really have hoped for a living, had marriage between them taken place.

By the beginning of 1779 Martha and Lord Sandwich had lived together, very happily, for over eighteen years and she had borne him nine children, five of which had survived. In March 1779, Martha decided to end the relationship with Hackman. She certainly didn't balk at the idea of a respectable marriage but at the risk of losing her children, it was a step she was not prepared to take. Instead, she determined to continue to live the happy existence she was accustomed to with her children and their ageing father; after all Lord Sandwich doted on his mistress and their children and she lived in the lap of luxury and was received in society. Despite Hackman's youthfulness, life in a country parsonage would not have held many attractions, considering what Martha Reay had become accustomed to.

On the day of the tragic event, 7 April 1779, Hackman dined with his sister and brother-in-law, who was also his first cousin. The couple had married only five weeks previously. He left them promising he would return for supper. That evening Lord Sandwich was working late at the Admiralty. Hackman, on seeing his lordship's coach with Martha Reay inside, concluded, quite correctly, that Miss Reay was going out to the opera, and would probably

The Reverend James Hackman. Author's collection

call on Signora Galli at her lodgings in the Haymarket (Catherina Galli was a retired *prima donna,* who amongst other fine singers had given Martha lessons. It was said that Martha Reay possessed a singing voice that could have earned her a high income, had she chosen a career on the stage). Hackman walked to the Cannon Coffee House, Charing Cross, where he expected to see Miss Reay pass, which he did indeed observe within a short time. He followed the carriage to Covent Garden, and saw Miss Reay and Signora Galli alight from it and go into the theatre. He followed the two ladies into the theatre and there observed a gentleman talking to Miss Reay. He was of a genteel and handsome appearance, and was later discovered to be Lord Coleraine. Hackman was seized with a fit of jealousy and at that moment decided to end his own life.

He left the theatre, went to his lodgings in Duke's Court, St Martin's Lane and returned a little while later with a brace of loaded pistols, intending to kill himself in the presence of the woman he loved. When questioned later why he had a brace of pistols, he replied that if one misfired on himself, he meant to use the other. When the play was over Martha Reay, in the company of Signora Galli and Lord Coleraine, whom Hackman had taken for his rival, entered the lobby of the theatre, and it was there that Hackman first attempted to shoot himself, but the thickness of the crowd prevented him. He kept Miss Reay in view, until she was under the canopy in the piazza, on her way to her coach. He tried a second time to shoot himself, but a chairman, running suddenly against him, almost pushed him to the ground. Hackman recovered his composure and pursued Miss Reay to the door of her coach, Signora Galli was already seated inside it. It was not until he beheld Martha Reay's face that he thought of killing her at that instant. He said that he decided it would be best for both to die together. He took a pistol from each pocket and stepping between Miss Reay and a gentleman, later identified as Mr Macnamara of Lincoln's Inn, who had held out his arm to assist Miss Reay in getting into her carriage, she being on his right hand, Hackman discharged the pistol in his right hand first, and immediately afterwards discharged the pistol in his left hand at himself. Miss Reay was shot through the head. She, upon lifting her hand to her face, fell and died on the spot; but finding himself alive after he had shot at himself, and fallen also with his feet close to those of Miss Reay, Hackman beat his head with the pistol and called out, Kill me! Kill me! The explosion of the pistol shots alarmed several gentlemen nearby, who, fearing for their lives, immediately

Tothill Fields Prison, where Hackman was initially imprisoned following his arrest. Author's collection

dispersed. Mr Macnamara was left for a few moments virtually alone amidst a scene of horror. Then several people came to his aid and Miss Reay was then carried to the Shakespeare Tavern and Hackman with her. Miss Reay's lifeless body was taken to a separate room within the tavern while Hackman's wounds were dressed in another. Hackman then enquired after Miss Reay and when he was told he had killed her he would not believe it, but said he was sure she was living, for that he only intended to kill himself. He freely gave his name and was shortly afterwards taken before the magistrate, Sir John Fielding (the celebrated blind magistrate, half-brother of lawyer and novelist Henry Fielding) who committed him to Tothill Fields Bridewell.

When the news was brought to Lord Sandwich late that night it was said:

> *His Lordship stood, as it were, petrified; till suddenly seizing a candle, he ran up stairs, and threw himself on the bed, and in an agony exclaimed, 'Leave me for a while to myself – I could have borne any thing but this.'*

The Reverend James Hackman was transferred to Newgate Gaol. During his incarceration in Newgate, Hackman remained calm and composed and it is said that he spoke of the name and memory of Martha Reay with the highest rapture. Hackman wrote to his brother-in-law:

> *I am alive – and she is dead. I shot her, shot her, and not myself. Some of her blood and brains is still upon my clothes. I don't ask you to speak to me, I don't ask you to look at me, only come hither and bring me a little poison, such as is strong enough. Upon my knees I beg, if your friendship for me ever was sincere, do, do bring me some poison.*

He had many visits from friends and family and he told them that, life since the lady was gone, would to him be a cruel punishment, and that death could only relieve him from a world wherein he should consider himself lost, since the only object that was dear to him was out of it, and whom he was thwarted on wholly possessing while in it.

On the morning of his trial at the Old Bailey Sessions, before Mr Justice Blackstone, Hackman ate a hearty breakfast in Newgate, with his brother-in-law, and two of his friends in attendance. One of the friends went with him to the court but his other friend and his brother-in-law were too distraught to attend. Hackman was said to be overcome by his feelings as witnesses against him were giving their evidence, his deportment was noble and it was said that this gained him much admiration by both judge and jury. The evidence of the prosecution having being presented, Hackman was asked if he had anything to say in his defence. Rising from his chair and wiping a flood of tears from his eyes, he sighed deeply, then delivered the following speech:

The Sessions House, Old Bailey, where Hackman was tried before Mr Justice Blackstone. Author's collection

My Lord. I should not have troubled the court with the examination of witnesses to support the charge against me, had I not thought that pleading guilty to the indictment would give an indication of contemning death, nor suitable to my present condition, and would, in some measure, make me accessory to a second peril of my life; and I likewise thought that the justice of my country ought to be satisfied, by suffering my offences to be proved, and the fact to be established by evidence.

I stand here the most wretched of human beings! I confess myself criminal in a high degree; I acknowledge with shame and repentance that my determination against my own life was formal and complete. I protest, with that regard to truth which becomes my situation, that the will to destroy her who was ever dearer to me than life, was never mine, until a momentary phrenzy [sic] overcame me, and induced me to commit the deed I deplore. – The letter which I meant for my brother-in-law after my decease, will have its due weight as to this point, with good men.

Before this dreadful act I trust nothing will be found in the tenor of my life, which the common charity of mankind will not readily excuse. I have no wish to avoid the punishment which the laws of my country appoint for my crime; but being already too unhappy to feel a punishment in death, or a satisfaction in life, I submit myself to the disposal and judgment of Almighty God, and to the consequences of the enquiry into my conduct and intention.

The letter, written on 7 April, which had been found in Hackman's pocket in the *Shakespeare Tavern* was then read out:

My Dear Frederick,

WHEN this reaches you I fhall be no more, but do not let my unhappy fate diftrefs you too much. I have ftrove againft it as long as poffible, but it now overpowers me. You know where my affections were placed; my having by fome means or other loft her's, (an idea which I could not fupport) has driven me to madnefs. The world will condemn me, but your good heart will pity me. God blefs you, my dear Fred. Would I had a fum to leave you, to convince you of my great regard. You was my only friend. I have hid one circumftance from you which gives me great pain: I owe Mr Wright, of Gofport, one hundred pounds, for which he has the writings opf my houfes; but I hope in God when they are fold, and all other matters collected, there will be nearly enough to fettle our account. May Almighty God blefs you and yours, with comfort and happinefs, and may you ever be a ftranger to the pangs I now feel. May heaven protect my beloved woman, and forgive this act which alone could relieve me from a world of mifery I have long endured. Oh! If it fhould be in your power to do her any act of friendship, remember your faithful friend,

J. HACKMAN.

A plea of insanity was attempted by his defence but this was not accepted. The Reverend James Hackman was found guilty of murder and sentenced to death. Following the verdict, Lord Sandwich wrote to Hackman:

17th April 1779

TO MR HACKMAN IN NEWGATE
If the murderer of Miss _____ wishes to live, the man he has most injured will use all his interest to procure his life.

Hackman sent an immediate reply:

The Condemned Cell in Newgate,
17th April 1779.

The murderer of her whom he preferred, far preferred to life, respects the hand from which he has just received such an offer as he neither desires nor deserves. His wishes are for death, not life. One wish he has. Could he be pardoned in this world by the man he has most injured – oh, my lord, when I meet her in another world enable me to tell her (if departed spirits are not ignorant of earthly things) that you forgive us both, that you will be a father to her dear infants!

J. H.

There was to be no reprieve or pardon for the Reverend James Hackman. Justice was swift, for there were only twelve days between the murder and the murderer's dissection. On 19 April 1779 Reverend James Hackman rose at 5 am, dressed himself, then spent some time in private contemplation. At 7 am, he was visited by some friends in the condemned cell, including James Boswell (1740–95, man of letters and friend and biographer of Dr Johnson), with whom he went to the chaplain and partook of the sacrament. On the journey from Newgate to Tyburn, Hackman was very subdued and spoke little. Boswell accompanied him in the mourning coach which a gentleman cleric was permitted to use instead of the usual cart to convey him to the place of execution. When he reached the dreaded triple tree, while waiting to be turned off, Hackman wrote a few last words in pencil:

My Dear Charlie,
farewell for ever in this world. I die a sincere Christian and Penitent, and everytimg I hope you can wish me. Would it prevent my example's having any bad effect if the world should know how I abhor my former ideas of suicide, my crime? ___ will be the best judge. Of her fame I charge you to be careful. My poorly will ...

Your dying H.

The noose having been placed around his neck, Hackman was turned off by hangman Edward Dennis, and life, having at last been pronounced extinct, much as Hackman had wished, his body was left hanging for the customary one hour, before being taken to Surgeon's Hall for dissection.

Here is a portion of a Grub Street ballad on the tragedy:

> A Sandwich favourite was this fair
> And her he dearly loved:
> By whom six children had, we hear:
> This story fatal proved.
>
> O Clergyman! O wicked one!
> In Covent Garden shot her.
> No time to cry upon her God-
> It's hoped He's not forgot her.
> Anonymous

Martha Reay was taken back to her native Hertfordshire, where she lies buried in Elstree.

CHAPTER 9

Assassination of the Prime Minister
1812

After the body had been allowed to hang for the customary hour it was taken down and loaded onto a cart, and conveyed, followed by a large crowd, to St Bartholomew's Hospital where it was dissected in the anatomical theatre before many spectators.

A t about a quarter past five on the evening of 11 May 1812, Prime Minister and First Lord of the Treasury, the Right Honourable Spencer Perceval, was on his way to the House of Commons. As the Prime Minister and his associates passed through the Lobby (which in the old houses of Parliament was opposite the south end of Westminster Hall), a thin-faced man, aged about forty, stepped forward, drew a pistol and shot the premier in the left breast. As the Prime Minister fell to the ground, he called out, 'Murder!'

The thin-faced man did not try to escape. When someone called out 'Shut the door; let no one out!' the man stood amidst the crowd that had gathered, and when a voice was heard to say, 'Who was the rascal that did it?' he came forward, still with the pistol in his hand, and said, 'I am the unfortunate man.' He was seized without resistance, and taken to the prison room of the Sergeant-at-Arms, where he was searched and questioned by several MPs. He had another pistol on his person, loaded and primed, and a copious bundle of letters and papers.

John Bellingham (top image). Bellingham shooting the Prime Minister in the Lobby of the House of Commons, 11 May 1812. Author's collection

Meanwhile, Lord Osborne and Mr W Smith, the member for Norwich, who were walking behind the Prime Minister when the shot was fired, lifted the injured Premier and carried him into the nearby office of the Speaker's secretary, where he shortly died.

Spencer Perceval (1762–1812) was born in London. He was called to the bar in 1786 and became an MP in 1796. He was appointed Solicitor General in 1801 and Attorney General in 1802. From 1807 until 1809, when he succeeded the Duke of Portland as Prime Minister, he served as Chancellor of the Exchequer. At the time of his death, the Tory government, which he led, was firmly established.

The assassin was taken to the bar of the House of Commons, where General Gascoyne, MP for Liverpool recognized him as John Bellingham, a former constituent, a man who had recently been a frequent visitor to the Commons, and from whom Gascoyne had received several petitions and memoranda, concerning his grievances with the Government over injustices he said he had received in Russia. It later became apparent that Bellingham had been seen in numerous lobbies and corridors and had made enquiries as to the identities of various Members. When asked what his motive was for shooting the Prime Minister, Bellingham replied:

It was want of redress and denial of justice on the part of the government.

John Bellingham grew up in London and worked for merchants in the Russian trade. He was sent on business to Archangel, where he remained for three years. On his return to England, he married a Miss Nevill, and when the opportunity arose to go to Archangel again, he took his wife with him, in 1804. In Archangel, Bellingham found himself involved in a complicated business dispute, which, apparently, through no fault of his own, left him in debt to some Russian merchants, in the sum of 2,000 roubles (about £200). He also faced a criminal suit in which he alleged in a letter that fraudulent transactions had taken place regarding the placement of insurance on certain ships' cargoes. What he had intended to be a short visit was to last almost five years. He was detained in several prisons, at various times and on his release ordered to remain in Russia until the 2,000 roubles had been paid. He received help from the British Ambassador to Russia, Lord Granville Leveson-Gower and finally obtained permission to return to England in May 1809, where he became engaged in business in Liverpool, as an insurance broker. However, his experiences in Russia seemed to have unbalanced his mind and he became obsessed with receiving compensation for the British

Ambassador to Russia's failure to adequately defend his rights there. He wrote letters to the Privy Council. These letters were ultimately passed on to the Treasury, for the attention of the Chancellor of the Exchequer, who was at that time Spencer Perceval. Bellingham was clearly made aware of this, as, when Perceval chose to ignore them, and politely turned him down, Bellingham turned his attention to the local MP, General Gascoyne, who likewise chose to ignore Bellingham's persistent requests. Bellingham even wrote to the Prince of Wales, who referred the letters to the Treasury.

After three years of failure to secure the compensation he believed he was entitled to, Bellingham moved to London. He wrote a letter to the magistrates at Bow Street Police Court:

Sirs, - I much regret it being my lot to have to apply to your worships under most peculiar and novel circumstances. For the particulars of the case I refer to the enclosed letter of Mr Secretary Ryder, the notification from Mr Perceval, and my petition to Parliament, together with the printed papers herewith. The affair requires no further remark than that I consider his Majesty's Government to have completely endeavoured to close the door of justice, in declining to have, or even permit, my grievances to be brought before Parliament for redress, which privilege is the birthright of every individual. The purport of the present is, therefore, once more to solicit his Majesty's Ministers, through your medium, to let what is right and proper be done in my instance, which is all I require. Should this reasonable request be finally denied, I shall then feel justified in executing justice myself – in which case I shall be ready to argue the merits of so reluctant a measure with his Majesty's Attorney-General, wherever and whenever I may be called upon to do so. In the hopes of averting so abhorrent but compulsive an alternative I have the honour to be, sirs, your very humble and obedient servant,

John Bellingham
9 New Millman Street
March 23 1812

Less than two months later Bellingham decided to bring his grievances to the attention of a wider audience and purchased a pair of pistols.

Bellingham's trial took place at the Sessions House, Old Bailey, on 15 May 1812, just four days after Perceval's death, before Lord Chief Justice Mansfield. A commentator wrote:

The judges at ten o'clock took their seats on each side of the Lord Mayor; and the recorder, the Duke of Clarence, the Marquis Wellesley and almost all the aldermen of the City of London occupied the bench. The Court was crowded to excess, and no distinction of rank was observed, so that Members of the House of Commons were forced to mingle with the throng. There were also present a great number of ladies, all led by the most intense curiosity to behold the assassin, and to hear what he might urge in defence or palliation of his atrocious act.

Bellingham made a speech to the jury and rambled on for two hours. Although it appears by his actions that Bellingham was insane, and some witnesses said as much at the trial; and certainly many who have studied the case believe that to be so, he apparently showed no visible signs of insanity, at least not in the conventional sense of madness, as perceived at that time. Unless a person was obviously out of his mind, then a jury would have no alternative but to find a prisoner guilty, if they believed he had committed the crime for which he was being tried. Clearly in Bellingham's case, when the judge asked the jury to consider if the prisoner was able to distinguish good from evil, right from wrong, they believed he was, because after just fourteen minutes of deliberation, they returned with a 'Guilty' verdict, and Bellingham was sentenced to death.

John Bellingham was executed outside Newgate Gaol, before an enormous crowd on the following Monday. The executioner was William Brunskill. During the long wait for the prisoner to be brought out, several members of the public were injured, caused by the goring by a maddened, over-driven ox, which forced its way through the crowd.

When the time came, Bellingham made his way from the condemned cell to the scaffold, which he ascended with a 'rather light step, a cheerful countenance and a confident, calm, but not exulting air'. After the body had been allowed to hang for the customary hour, it was taken down and loaded onto a cart, and conveyed, followed by a large crowd, to St Bartholomew's Hospital where it was dissected in the anatomical theatre before many spectators.

Not everyone was content with Bellingham's fate, as this contemporary account shows:

Bellingham has been convicted of murder and hanged, but some unease is now felt, since his wits had apparently been turned by the wrongs he suffered, and it is not the mark of a civilized society to execute lunatics.

Spencer Perceval is the only British Prime Minister to have been assassinated.

CHAPTER 10

The Cato Street Conspiracy
1820

*After the men had been hanged, their bodies were
taken down and their heads removed by a masked man
wielding a surgeon's knife. The severed heads were
each in turn displayed to the crowds of onlookers.*

Travelling in a northerly direction from Marble Arch along Edgeware Road, on the right hand side, after about a quarter of a mile, is Harrowby Street. Second left off Harrowby Street is a narrow road known as Cato Street, famous for what is known to history as the 'Cato Street Conspiracy of 1820'. The plot was given that name because the conspirators met in a loft above a stable at No.6. This ill-conceived plot seemed doomed to failure from the start and is probably more notable for the high profile execution of the perpetrators, than the actual purpose of the conspiracy itself. It nevertheless caused quite a stir at the time. The

The stable in Cato Street and a floor plan of the room above in which the conspirators met.
Author's collection

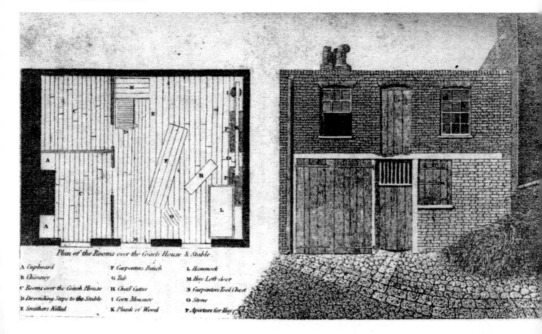

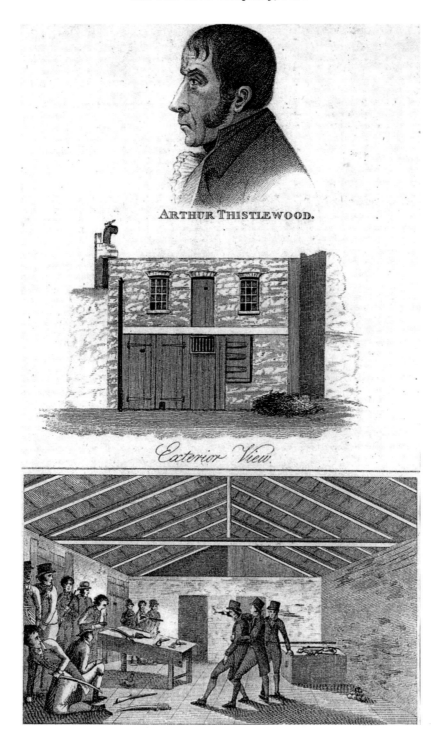

ARTHUR THISTLEWOOD.

Exterior View.

Arthur Thistlewood and the stable in which the Cato Street Conspirators met. Author's collection

plot involved a group of extreme radicals who were highly dissatisfied with government legislature, in the wake of the Napoleonic wars, a time when economic problems and high unemployment were rife.

The leader, Arthur Thistlewood, was a militia officer, who following visits to America and France, developed revolutionary sympathies and on 15 November 1816, had organized a demonstration at Spa Fields, intending to seize the Tower of London and the Bank of England. Thistlewood was arrested along with several others and tried before the King's Bench at Westminster, on 9 June. He was acquitted. When Thistlewood began to recruit at Cato Street, he secured the support of about twenty-five men, including many hot-headed illiterates. One of the recruits was a government spy, named George Edwards, so the authorities were aware of the plot from the beginning. Edwards probably joined the conspirators for personal gain and immediately after joining the group, went straight to Windsor to inform Sir Herbert Taylor. The conspirators planned to murder Lord Liverpool, the Prime Minister and his entire cabinet, while they dined at Lord Harrowby's (the President of the Council) house at 29 Grosvenor Square, on 23 February 1820. Another conspirator, Thomas Hiden, also turned informer and gave the government exact details of the plot. The plot involved one of the conspirators to knock at the door of Lord Harrowby's residence on the pretence of leaving a parcel. When the door was opened the whole band of men would rush into the house and, while a few took care of the servants, the others would fall upon Lord Harrowby and his guests. Hand-grenades were to be thrown into the dining room and during the noise and confusion the assassination of the entire cabinet would be accomplished.

RICHARD TIDD.   WILLIAM DAVIDSON

THOMAS BRUNT   JAMES INGS

Thistlewood and others were closely watched and once matters were sufficiently advanced so as no doubt could remain as to their guilt, a detachment of soldiers, headed by Lord Frederick Fitzclarence, constables and Bow Street officials descended on Cato Street. During the ensuing fracas, Thistlewood killed one of the officers, Richard Smithers, with his sword, then promptly took to his heels and escaped.

The four Cato Street Conspirators who were executed with Arthur Thistlewood on 1 May 1820. Author's collection

The stable in which the Cato Street Conspirators met, seen here, September 2005. The author

Several others conspirators were captured and taken to Bow Street: Richard Bradburn, Charles Cooper, William Davidson, James Gilchrist, James Ings, John Monument, John Shaw Strange and Richard Tidd. A large number of weapons was found in the loft and taken away. Thistlewood was caught the next day at 8 White Street, Little Moorfields, to the north of the present day Moorgate station. He was in bed with his breeches on and in the pockets were found several cartridges. He was first taken to Bow Street, where he was examined and then appeared before the Privy Council. Other conspirators including John Thomas Brunt and John Harrison were arrested over the next few days. Thistlewood was taken to the Tower of London as State prisoners with his fellow ringleaders but most of the other conspirators were held in Coldbath Fields Prison.

Six weeks after the proposed assassination of the cabinet, the trial of the Cato Street Conspirators took place at the Old Bailey. Thistlewood made a long and rambling defence. He also described the 'informer' George Edwards as a 'contriver, instigator and entrapper'. It came as no surprise that the prisoners were all found guilty. Those conspirators who had pleaded guilty escaped execution but five were executed.

Thistlewood, Ings, Davidson, Brunt and Tidd were hanged outside Newgate Gaol on 1 May 1820. The five conspirators were spared

being disembowelled and quartered
but the law still required traitors to be
decapitated. Arthur Griffiths records
in *The Chronicles of Newgate:*

*A crowd as great as any known
collected in the Old Bailey to see the
ceremony, about which there were some
peculiar features worth recording. The
reckless demeanour of all the convicts
except Davidson was most marked.
Thistlewood and Ings sucked oranges on
the scaffold; they with Brunt and Tidd
scorned the ordinary's ministrations,
but Ings said he hoped God would be
more merciful to him than men had
been. Ings was especially defiant. He
sought to cheer Davidson, who seemed
affected, crying out, "Come, old cock-of-
wax, it will soon be over." As the
executioner fastened the noose, he
nodded to a friend he saw in the crowd;
and catching sight of the coffins ranged
around the gallows, he smiled at the
show with contemptuous indifference.*

The execution of the Cato Street Conspira[...]
outside the Debtor's Entrance at Newgate G[...]
Author's collection

*He roared out snatches of a song about
Death or Liberty, and just before he was turned off, yelled out three cheers
to the populace whom he faced. He told the executioner to "do it tidy," to
pull it tight, and was in a state of hysterical exaltation up to the very last.
Davidson, who was the only one who seemed to realize his awful
situation, listened patiently and with thankfulness to the chaplain, and
died in a manner strongly contrasting with that of his fellows …*

After the men had been hanged, their bodies were taken down after
half an hour and their heads removed by a masked man wielding a
surgeon's knife. The severed heads were each in turn displayed to the
crowds of onlookers. Afterwards the bodies were placed in the
coffins, with the heads in the correct position and taken inside
Newgate Gaol, where they were buried in the narrow passage which
linked the gaol with the adjoining Sessions House, officially known
as Birdcage Walk, on account of it being open to the air but covered

The scene outside Newgate Gaol during high profile public executions. Author's collection

with an iron grid; but more commonly known as Dead Man's Walk. There carved in the stones was a row of letters T, B, I, D and T, for Thistlewood, Brunt, Ings, Davidson and Tidd, to mark the spot where they were buried. This was the fashion at Newgate. In all there were ninety-seven such burials there. When Newgate was demolished in 1903, the remains of all ninety-seven executed criminals were lifted and reburied in the City of London Cemetery. George Edwards, it was said, after the conviction of the conspirators had been assured, went abroad, with an ample pension, provided on condition he did not return to England.

CHAPTER 11

Murder at the Adelphi
1897

*Mad? Mad? You will hear of my madness. The whole
world will ring with it.*

*"Shadows we are, and shadows we pursue",
That was the motto dearest far to you!
Old friend and comrade, having grasped my hand,
I mourn you lost to me in Shadow Land.*

*Brave Sailor Lad! And best of "pals" on earth,
Whose triumph at your death, proclaimed your worth,
They bore you down an avenue of woe,
Where men and women sobbed, "We loved him so!"*

*Why did they love him? The assassin's knife,
With one fell blow, mangled a loyal life,
They loved him for his honour! Splendid Will!
That made a hero of our "BREEZY BILL!"*

Punch, January 1898

London's theatreland has had a rich and varied history, and
by the very nature of things theatrical, has attracted such
diverse personalities and social classes it has often been the
scene of crime, sometimes murder. This particular theatrical murder
is one of the most sensational true-life theatrical tragedies, which
made headline news. For the following five years or so, the crime
around which this tragic series of events is based, was used by
theatrical journalists to moralize about the theatrical profession. The
victim was one of the most distinguished figures and celebrated
actors of his day. This is the tale of a practical joke that went seriously
wrong, of baseless jealousy arising from another actor's cruel hoax.
The scene of the murder was the Adelphi Theatre in the Strand, in
1897. At that time both the Strand and the adjacent Adelphi were

William Terriss, wearing a soft brimmed hat. Author's collection

highly fashionable areas, much more so than the present day. The Strand itself, was the hubbub of London's high society and theatrical activity.

The principal players in this tragic tale are William Terriss (William Charles James Lewin), the actor and murder victim; Richard Archer Prince, a supernumerary, stagehand and the murderer; and William L Abingdon, actor and the perpetrator of the joke that turned sour.

William Terriss was affectionately known by the British public as 'Breezy Bill' and 'No.1, Adelphi Terriss' (Adelphi Terrace being one of London's most fashionable streets), and was noted for wearing a soft brimmed hat, which was considered old fashioned. Although not an actor manager, such was his standing that he was treated with the same respect as if he were, throughout the theatrical world. He was one of the kindest and most generous of men. Handsome, athletic and an accomplished swimmer, he rescued several people from drowning and once turned up at the theatre soaking wet, having rescued a drowning man from the Serpentine, shrugging the matter off, as if of no consequence. When he was living at Barnes he rescued several people from the Thames and during a holiday at Deal, whilst in a rowing boat with his son, Tom, he came across three youths in difficulty and rescued them. As a result he received the medal of the Royal Humane Society.

William Charles James Lewin was born on 20 February 1847 in St Johns Wood, London. His family was affluent and well connected. His father, George Lewin, a well-known barrister, died when William was ten. He had two older brothers, Thomas Herbert and Friend (his mother's maiden name). William had by the age of sixteen already left four schools. A letter written to his brother in about 1859 when he was twelve, gives an insight into his schooldays.

Windermere College
Westmoreland

My Dear Friend:
We have begun cricket, and I am in the fifth eleven. I have a good lot of
marbles, and I have a nice little flask. I don't think I told you that I had
a fight with Farie, a new fellow, about as big as Rushton, and Jip Gibson
was my second; and I think I fought very well, considering you were not
there. Jump and Morty backed me, and I nearly got my head broken. I
wish you had been there. I am getting on pretty well, and how are you?
Is your tutor a good one?

Love to all,
And believe me,
My dear brother,
Your affectionate Brother,
WILLIE

Write soon

Possessing a spirit for wandering, when it was suggested that he be
entered for the Merchant Navy, William jumped at the chance. At the
age of sixteen the firm of Green and Co. took him on and provided
him with a uniform, which he relished wearing. His naval career did
not last for long, in total just two weeks. Embarking at Gravesend
and being seen off by members of his family, he jumped ship at
Portsmouth and arrived back at the family home, then at 6 Talbot
Square, Bayswater. His next seafaring expedition saw him
accompanying his godfather John Henry Graves on a Mediterranean
voyage. On his return he tried his hand at medicine and engineering.
Neither of these suited him. He looked for excitement and found it
on the stage.

At the age of seventeen, Terriss inherited a legacy from his uncle.
He bought extravagant things including a carriage, which he had
designed himself. The money was soon spent, so his family decided
that he should go to India, where his brother Thomas was Deputy
Commissioner of Chittagong. Terriss was sent to Assam, where he
became a tea planter. He did not take to it and was soon on his way
back to England. His family encouraged him to take up engineering.
However, this did not suit him, nor did medicine, a profession which
his brother, Friend, had entered. At this time Friend Lewin was

working as a houseman at St Mary's Hospital, Paddington. Terriss became a member of the hospital's Rugby Football Club and also of the Dramatic Society. After he had dabbled in amateur theatre he made his first professional appearance at the 'Prince of Wales', Birmingham in the 1867–68 season. He adopted the name William Terriss, which he chose from a street directory. This engagement saw Terriss doubling for the leading man in a difficult escape scene from Dion Boucicault's melodrama, *Arrah-na-Pogue*. This led to a speaking role, the part of Chowser, in Boucicault's thriller *The Flying Scud*. From these small beginnings, Terriss decided it was time to try his hand on the London stage. With that end in sight he went to St. John's Wood, where opposite his old home lived the leading lights of the new drama on the London stage, Squire and Marie Bancroft. Bancroft's account of his first meeting with Terriss explains the young man's enthusiasm and determination to secure an engagement:

During the previous summer we were constantly told by a maidservant that "a young gentleman had called" who seemed very persistent about

seeing us. One day, returning from a walk, the girl informed me that "the young gentleman" had pushed past her and walked into our little drawing-room, where he then was. I joined our visitor rather angrily, but was soon disarmed by the frank manner of a very young man, who, within five minutes, in the course of conversation, pointed to the window of a house opposite and said, "That's the room I was born in" … Of course "the young gentleman" was stage-struck, and "wanted to go on the stage", adding that "he was resolved we should give him an engagement". His courage, and if I may say it, his cool perseverance, amused and amazed me; the very force of his determined manner conquered me, and the upshot of our interview was that I did engage him. His name was William

Sir Squire Bancroft. Author's collection

Terriss, and Lord Cloudwrays, in Society, *was the part in which he made his first appearance on a London stage.*

Terriss was not an immediate success and he grew impatient for excitement. He married the actress Amy Fellowes (given name Isabel Lewis) in 1870, and he and his wife decided to emigrate to the Falkland Islands, where he became a sheep farmer and horse breeder and breaker in. Shortly before he decided to return home in 1871, his wife gave birth to a daughter, Ellaline on 13 April 1871. She blossomed into a great beauty and highly successful actress, of whom her father was very proud. She married the actor manager Seymour Hicks (knighted 1935). Sir Seymour died in 1949 at the age of seventy-eight. Ellaline, Lady Hicks lived until 1971, dying three months after her hundredth birthday. On his arrival back in England, Terriss was engaged once again by the Bancrofts and met with success. His wife never acted again. His reputation grew and he made his name as Squire Thornhill in *Olivia* at the Court Theatre in 1878, playing opposite Ellen Terry. It was said of Terriss that he possessed a charm and a smile which few women could resist and all men envied. Terriss played Romeo opposite Adelaide Neilson's Juliet, and then in 1880 joined Henry Irving at the Lyceum, where he remained for some time. Irving had great respect for Terriss, who was one of the few actors who dared to stand up to him. In her book *Exits And Entrances,* the actress Eva Moore recalled:

*WILLIAM TERRISS.- "Breezy Bill Terriss", the hero of the Adelphi dramas. Handsome, lovable, with a tremendous breadth of style in his acting that we see too seldom in these days of "restraint". His Henry VIII to Irving's Wolsey was a magnificent piece of acting. There is a story told of him, when Irving was rehearsing a play in which there was a duel –*The Corsican Brothers, *I think. At the dress rehearsal ("with lights" to represent the moon, which lit the fight), Irving called to "the man in the moon": "Keep it on me, on me!" Terriss dropped his sword: "Let the moon shine on me a little," he begged; "Nature is at least impartial."*

In October 1882, the actress Jessie Millward appeared as Hero at the Lyceum Theatre in *Much Ado About Nothing.* Terriss played Claudio in the production. Three years after this, in December 1885, they made a name for themselves as a romantic couple in *Harbour Lights* by Sims and Pettitt. Afterwards this successful team often appeared in the same productions and they toured Britain and America. She became his mistress, although Terriss and his wife continued to have a very happy life together. Terriss came into his own when he embarked on a famous series of melodramas at the Adelphi, in September 1894, with Jessie Millward as his leading lady (he called her 'Sis' and she referred to him as 'my comrade'), elevating him to the foremost exponent in this field.

Richard Archer Prince was born in Dundee. At his trial, his age was given as thirty-two, but his mother maintained that he was her eldest son born in 1858. This would have made him thirty-nine. In any event, he looked considerably older than his years. One significant fact, which was to manifest itself in Prince's psyche, was that there were strains of madness on his father's side. One half-brother was born insane and another died in a lunatic asylum. Richard Archer (he adopted the name of Prince later, because he thought that name was more becoming of a future great actor), was short of stature, with a slight cast in his right eye and a heavy, dark, droopy moustache, which he waxed at both ends. He dressed eccentrically, and often wore the attire associated with a stage villain. Sometimes he wore a long cape and invariably a slouch hat. Many of his acquaintances simply regarded him as a harmless eccentric. Others, who perhaps saw deeper into his psyche, rightly nicknamed him 'Mad Archer'.

He had a wretched, poverty-stricken childhood, and nurtured a burning ambition to become a great actor. He was apprenticed to a Dundee shipbuilder but spent his spare time and money at the Theatre Royal. Sometime later he secured a walk-on part, swelling the ranks of a visiting company. This was the beginning of his undistinguished theatrical career. Early in his career Richard Archer's strange and sudden outbursts got him the nickname Mad Archer. His sister, Maggie, moved south to London, where she became a lady of easy virtue. She was a frequenter of the notorious Empire Promenade (the promenade gallery of the famous Empire Theatre), a place where gentleman used to go to meet ladies of dubious character. One of her regular gentleman friends was the actor William L Abingdon. Richard Archer Prince found his way to London in 1881. He sought out his sister, who it is believed sweet-talked her beau, Billy Abingdon, to secure her brother some employment. One of Billy Abingdon's nightly customs was to entertain Maggie Archer in his dressing-room and he sometimes invited her brother to join them. It was during these nightly visits that, to quote Seymour Hicks:

"Mr. A" discovered that the poor half-wit from the North was possessed of a wild desire to reach impossible heights.

Had Billy Abingdon been aware of Prince's state of mental health, all who knew him feel sure he would not have taken the steps he did and put into that diseased mind the idea that Terriss was the one man who stood in the way of his greatness. The general consensus was that there was no malicious intention in Abingdon's mind, merely the idea that a great deal of fun might be provided for himself and his chums at the expense of a deluded and inflated buffoon.

Prince's first London engagement was at the Adelphi in *Michael Strogoff,* in 1881. He continued to appear as a super or in minor roles, mostly in the provinces, for several years. In spite of this, he believed that given the right opportunity, he would immediately establish himself as the truly 'great actor' he felt in his twisted mind that he undoubtedly was. Prince may have worked on productions in which Terriss was appearing before he was engaged in *Harbour Lights*. It was during the run of *Harbour Lights*, which opened in December 1885, that Terriss caused Prince to be sacked after he had made an offensive remark against him. However, Terriss helped Prince out on several occasions by sending him money when he was out of work. Prince often wrote begging letters to Terriss and other leading actors, and Terriss was not unsympathetic to those who were less well placed than himself in the profession. A fellow 'super' in *Harbour Lights* was C St

John Denton. He later became an agent, and in the years that followed, up until Prince slayed Terriss, Denton was often visited by Prince in his search for work. Denton recalled that when he joined the *Harbour Lights* company:

> *I understood he had been there some time. Indeed we looked on him as a "standing dish". He dressed in the same room with me … I had ample opportunity of noting his eccentricities … He had a brogue that you could cut …*

Prince often found himself working in menial jobs outside the theatrical profession, when he was

William Terriss and William L Abingdon in The Fatal Card, *1894.* Author's collection

unable to secure gainful employment in any capacity within the theatre. *The Silver Falls* opened in December 1888 and Prince was in the cast. His name appeared on the bill as 'Diego', although the character wasn't a speaking part. After the run ended Terriss left the Adelphi for five years. He went on a tour of America (1889–90) and Prince found himself out of work. However it was as 'R A Prince, late Adelphi Theatre' that he presented himself to potential employers. He established a connection with the provincial manager J F Elliston, a reputable manager who was based in Bolton, Lancashire. A production which Elliston found very profitable was *The Union Jack*, one of the most popular productions that had been staged at the Adelphi. Elliston regularly revived it and during the early 1890s Prince found himself appearing in the small role of the Sergeant. He also appeared in other plays for Elliston. Elliston kept a regular bunch of actors employed, so when the news of Terriss's murder broke, several of Prince's former colleagues came forward and expressed their opinion of him. One comment ran:

> *He thought himself a great actor, simply because once or twice he got a couple of lines to speak. 'My lord, the carriage waits', and that class of work. Wanity, disappointed wanity and ambition – that's what I calls the reason of it.*

Prince stayed with Elliston's company for several seasons until the end of the 1894–95 tour. After this Prince was unable to find work, so he returned to Dundee where he obtained a job at an ironworks. The foreman, David Simpson, gave evidence at the trial and said Prince was a good worker. He also said that Prince was often violent, that he was called soft and that he once saw him foam at the mouth. However, Prince conducted himself quite differently outside the ironworks. He often visited Her Majesty's Theatre, where he would present himself with credentials which associated him with the Adelphi Theatre, and claim a seat in the best part of the house. He was often badly or eccentrically dressed, would often call out to the artistes, or applaud them in inappropriate places. It was reported in the *Dundee Advertiser* after the trial that on one occasion of members of the theatre staff:

> *… having eventually to carry him from the dress-circle and expel him from the building" because Prince had uttered threats to shoot one of the actors and brandished a revolver.*

Prince began writing abusive and threatening letters to numerous theatrical figures accusing them of 'blackmailing' him. He uses this expression many times and presumably meant 'blackballing'. His former employer JF Elliston received a letter which ran:

You hell-hound. You Judas. You have got me out of engagements by blackmailing me to get on yourself. You cur. I am not a woman. You hound, how dare you blackmail a Highlander? Next time I ask you for a reference, it will be at Bow Street Police Station, where my lawyer will expose you. If I die at Newgate, you will be to blame. I would advise you to take this letter to Scotland Yard this time. Victory or death is my motto, and the fear of God.

I am,
RICHARD ARTHUR (sic) PRINCE

Prince sent similar abusive letters to many managers and actors, including Terriss, over several years, usually when he was down on his luck. Towards the end of 1895 Prince returned to London, where he secured an engagement as a super in Seymour Hick's *One of the Best*, opening on 21 December. Terriss was leading man. During this engagement the cruel practical joke which resulted in such tragic consequences was formulated. Abingdon, who also appeared in a principal role in the play, and a couple of his cronies, found Prince's inflated opinion of himself quite hilarious. On Abingdon's instigation they encouraged his caprices, adding fuel to spark the fire of hatred, already smouldering and soon to burn ferociously in Prince's twisted brain. Together, they convinced Prince that in their opinion he had true greatness and he only needed the right opportunity to claim the laurel wreaths which were rightly his. Abingdon went so far as to secure a copy of Terriss's part for Prince to learn. At that time actors were not given the entire play script, simply their cue lines and part. Abingdon and his cronies arranged to have use of the stage during the day, where they watched with stifled laughter as Prince strutted the boards, spouting the lines of a part, they told him, with his talent, he should be playing … The seeds of hatred had been sown. Terriss was totally oblivious of the trouble which was brewing inside that diseased brain.

Seymour Hicks made reference to these events:

To please Prince, "Mr. A." had the part of the hero, the part Terriss was playing, typed for him to learn, and indeed went so far as to have what to him was a comic rehearsal called, and with the assistance of the extra people in the piece, had a hilarious hour watching the miserable weakling make a complete jackass of himself.

In his twisted brain Prince convinced himself that the only person who stood in the way of his success was William Terriss. Since Terriss caused him to be sacked from *Harbour Lights* all those years before Prince had held a grudge. In reality Terriss hardly new Prince and in spite of his generosity towards him, it seems unlikely that their relationship was one based on speaking terms. Prince considered himself to be at the very least Terriss's equal. All he needed was the right opportunity to prove his worth. William Terriss was his only rival. Without Terriss on the scene, what could possibly prevent him from taking over as the greatest romantic actor on the English stage?

Seymour Hicks commented:

Prince's fellow-supers, with whom he dressed, little realizing on what thin ice they were travelling, encouraged him for their amusement to talk more grandiloquently than ever of what he would do, should his great day ever arrive.

William L Abingdon, or Billy Abingdon as he was known by his intimates, had joined the Adelphi company in 1887 during the run of *The Silver Falls* and had been largely in the employment of that company ever since. He played the villainous Squire Ellsworth to Terriss's Dudley Keppel in *One of the Best* (written by Seymour Hicks and George Edwardes). Abingdon's strength was playing villainous roles. Himself an attractive looking man, although not nearly so much as Terriss, he may have been envious of Terriss's good looks and casual air, as well as his great success and general popularity, after he on one occasion was not cast as a villain, he failed miserably. Sometime after Terriss's murder Abingdon moved to America where he enjoyed some success. In 1906, he married a well-known American actress, Bijou Fernandez. Her mother was an influential agent, who helped to secure Abingdon work. Eventually, the parts simply did not come Abingdon's way and in time the marriage failed. He died by his own hand in 1918.

Described by Seymour Hicks in *Between Ourselves:*

"Mr. A" I knew well. He was a capital actor and a pleasant enough companion, though by no means possessed of any particularly attractive

qualities. Perhaps it was for this latter reason that he was always cast as the villain in whatever play he appeared in at the old Adelphi. This being so, it can be readily understood that his work in no way clashed with that of the darling hero of the gods, William Terriss, but notwithstanding, his jealousy of my father-in-law knew no bounds, and he took little pains to sneer in company at the position of his brother-actor held in the affection of the public.

Hicks goes on to say:

Outwardly to Terriss, "Mr. A" was agreeable and hail-fellow-well-met, but behind his back he never lost an opportunity of belittling the man who, himself being of the most frank and charming disposition, was quite unconscious of the venom which lurked behind the smile of the man he looked upon as a good comrade.

One of the Best closed and Prince's services were not required in the following play. This may have caused him a great deal of anguish, if not resentment, as the play which followed *One of the Best,* had a large requirement for supers. *Boys Together* had battle scenes in Egypt and Sudan, and Prince would have been more than suitable as a 'type' for the play. Perhaps his previous behavior went against him. He sent several begging letters to various actors, including Terriss, who sent him money. By the summer of 1896 Prince's situation was becoming desperate. Unable to find work, he ventured north to his hometown, Dundee, where he obtained work at the Wallace Foundry, which he left after he managed to secure a theatrical engagement. The company was under the management of Arthur Carlton, of the Crown Theatre, Stoke-on-Trent. Carlton had sent out a tour of *The Union Jack.* During its run at the Grand Theatre, Glasgow, a member of the cast dropped out and an emergency replacement was required. Prince impressed the management sufficiently with his connection with London's famous Adelphi Theatre and that combined with the fact that he had toured with *The Union Jack* secured him the job. Prince was engaged to play the part of the chief villain, Sir Philip Yorke. That character, although himself the pivot of most of the disasters in the play, is himself being blackmailed by Captain Morton. Morton knows that Sir Philip is a forger. The climax of the role played by Prince has him stabbing his blackmailer:

MORTON: *(seeing the knife)* What have you there?
YORKE: Give me that bill!
MORTON: Madman! *(gripping YORKE)*
YORKE: *(lifting the knife)* By Heaven, I'll have it or I'll murder you! Give it to me!
MORTON: No. *(struggle – YORKE stabs him)*

Prince's general behaviour and his inability to remember lines resulted in his dismissal when the company reached South Shields. By a stroke of luck, another manager found himself in desperate need. Ralph Croydon was assembling a company in nearby Newcastle-upon-Tyne. Prince was duly engaged to play Sir Lester Lightfoot in *Nurse Charity* and Sir Geoffrey Dashwood in *Parson Thorn*. Prince was engaged for twenty-five shillings a week. And so began what was to become Prince's last, shortest and best documented engagement. The company were due to open at Hetton, two days later. At rehearsals it was soon apparent that Prince was incapable of carrying out his duties. He was unable to remember lines and behaved oddly. Before the end of the first day of rehearsals Ralph Croydon dismissed him. Prince asked Croydon to give him more time and to cancel the first performance. When Croydon refused, Prince replied:

I have now got two enemies: one here, one at the Adelphi.

Croydon remonstrated with Prince and emphasised the respect in which Terriss was held throughout the profession. Prince answered:

Fools often succeed where men of genius fail.

The next day Prince turned up at Croydon's lodgings, returning another four times, to beg for his wages. Croydon refused to give him anything and dismissed him as a madman. Prince's riposte was swift:

Mad? Mad? You will hear of my madness. The whole world will ring with it.

Prince made his way back to London by sea. It was reported that of the many and various jobs which Prince took between theatrical engagements, that he had served as a ship's steward and also as a valet. Short of money, he may have used his contacts to secure his passage. After Prince's arrest it was discovered that his theatrical 'skip' had been pledged and was still lying at Trades Wharf, Wapping. Prince arrived in London on 28 October. He found lodgings in Eaton Court, Buckingham Palace Road – a room at three shillings a week, knocked down by his sympathetic landlady, Mrs Charlotte Darby, from four shillings.

Shortly after his arrival in London, Prince went to the business premises of Mr George Lauberg, a cutler in Brompton Road, where he purchased a knife for 9d. The proprietor remembered a man answering Prince's description buying a knife one evening towards the end of October. He also remembered he had tried to press a better quality knife on Prince at one shilling but Prince declined to buy it, saying he could not afford it. Prince also paid a visit to the stage door of the Adelphi Theatre on 9 November and asked the stage-doorkeeper, Henry Spratt, if a note could be sent to Mr Terriss. The note was taken to Terriss's dressing room and a reply returned to Prince. This took the form of a reference to the Actors' Benevolent Fund. It was later given in evidence. The note from Terriss, given to Prince out of the goodness of his heart, read:

I have known the bearer, R. A. Prince, as a hard-working actor ...

Prince made frequent requests to the Actors' Benevolent Fund. His begging letters were produced at his trial. One read:

To the Gentlemen of the Committee:

Gentlemen,
   The reason I have to ask for help is that I was out of an engagement for over 12 months before I received the last one, and lost it through no fault of my own. All the time I was in my last engagement, I had to spend all my money in dressing the parts of Captain Morton and Sir Philip Yorke. When I left off on Saturday night I had not a shilling to call my own. I have parted with everything I have in the world. My box is at the dock for my fare and passage. I have nowhere else to go. I thought I might get something to do in town. For the last six or seven years all the engagements I have had, it has taken the money I received from them to keep me on tour. It was taking me all my time to live without being able to save. If you will only help me to live for a week or two, I think I shall be able to get an engagement.

Yours faithfully,
Richard A. Prince

As time went by Princes appeals to the Committee of the Actors'
Benevolent Fund showed his increasing decline:

Dear Sir,
I shall not get an engagement in London now. You might ask the
gentlemen of the committee if they would kindly lend me a pound to take
me home. The ship goes today. After they have been so kind, they might
do this if you will ask. Thanking you for your kindness,

Yours faithfully
R. ARCHER PRINCE

In all the Committee of the Actors' Benevolent Fund made him four
payments, of £1, £1, 10/- and 10/-.

On 13 December Prince went to the Vaudeville Theatre, which was
under the same management as the Adelphi, presented his card and
demanded a complimentary ticket. When he was refused he became
extremely abusive and threatening and had to be physically ejected
from the building.

On the morning of 16 December, Prince left his lodgings, after
being refused hot water by Mrs Derby. He was behind with his rent
and she had had enough. He paid a final visit to the Actors'
Benevolent Fund, but was told that his application for assistance had
been rejected. He asked who had chaired the meeting and was told
Mr Terry (Fred Terry – the actor and light comedian. Perhaps Prince
mistook this for Terriss). It has been suggested that Prince murdered
Terriss by mistake and his intended victim was in fact Fred Terry, and
this story was widely circulated. Although Prince did write to Fred
Terry and to his wife Julia Neilson, after they had turned down a play
he had written. Fred Terry received the following letter from Prince:

Sir,
Please return play Countess Otho at once. If you are hard up for the
money will send it. Terriss, the Pope, Scotland Yard. I will answer in a
week.

And Terry's wife received the following:

Madam,
I thank you as a Highlander and a gentleman, in the name of the
Almighty God, our Queen, and my rights for play Countess Otho.

Shortly after Prince had made that final visit to the Actors' Benevolent Fund he went to see the agent C St John Denton, in Maiden Lane, seeking work. His visit proved fruitless. He walked into the Strand and by an unlucky chance, came face to face with his sister, Maggie. He asked her for money but after several years of such requests, and an increasing amount more recently, she replied 'I would rather see you dead in the gutter than give you a farthing.' This final rejection was too much for him. He walked back to Maiden Lane and positioned himself opposite the private entrance.

During this period Terriss had every reason to be pleased with himself. His company was to appear in a Command Performance on Christmas Eve, before the Queen, at Windsor Castle. The word was out, he was to be knighted. On 16 December Terriss was discussing moving from his West London home Bedford Park, in Turnham Green to a larger house in Maida Vale, with John Graves. They played poker with Fred Terry at the Green Room Club and afterwards went to Jessie Millward's flat in Prince's Street, Hanover Square. She provided them with a light meal and left them playing chess. Miss Millward recalled:

> *When seven o'clock came I rose: "I must go down to the theatre," I said. "I hate being rushed," and left them finishing their game of chess. I drove up in my hansom to the pass door in Maiden lane, which opened near my dressing-room. At the pass door I saw standing the man Prince, whom I recognized as a former super. Only a night or two previously I had heard a man speaking in a loud voice in Mr Terriss's dressing-room, and as I came out of my room I met him in the passage with Prince. I had asked him: "What is the matter?" "This man is becoming a*

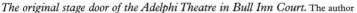

The original stage door of the Adelphi Theatre in Bull Inn Court. The author

nuisance," he had told me, and I had guessed it was a case of begging. Just as I reached the pass door Prince came towards me, and I half thought of giving him some money so that he should not delay Mr Terriss when he arrived, but as he came towards me there was something in the man's face that frightened me, and instead of waiting to open the pass door I rushed to the stage door, and on entering my dressing-room I told my maid, Lottie, of my encounter with Prince.

Terriss and his companion were dropped off at the end of Maiden Lane and walked the short distance to the private entrance. It was a little after seven o'clock. Terriss took the key from his pocket and, as he was bending to put the key in the lock, a figure emerged from across the narrow lane and hurriedly stabbed him twice in the upper back. These wounds were superficial. Indeed, Terriss's companion (John Henry Graves [Terriss's godfather, architect and lifelong friend]), took the blows to be in friendship. Terriss turned to confront his assailant and, in doing so received a third blow to the chest, which pierced his heart. Then, Terriss cried out 'My God! I am stabbed.' Graves, realising what had happened, took hold of Prince and held him until a constable arrived. Prince offered no resistance. Several passers by called out 'Murder!' and 'Police!'. The cries were heard by Police Constable Bragg. He was quickly on the scene and took Prince into custody on Graves' accusation. Sometime later Graves followed them to Bow Street, where he gave his evidence to Inspector French.

On hearing the commotion outside, and seeing something was amiss, Jessie Millward sped down the staircase. She found Terriss leaning against the wall, just inside the private entrance. Some years later in her autobiography, she described the scene:

The rear of the Adelphi Theatre, August 2005. The door on the right was the Royal Entrance, where members of the Royal family could gain access to their box without attracting attention, if they so wished. The present-day stage door is next to it and the 'Private Entrance' to the left, just before the sliding shutter of the scene dock.
The author

The 'Private Entrance' of the Adelphi Theatre in Maiden Lane, where William Terriss was fatally stabbed. The plaque, unveiled by Sir Donald Sinden, exactly a hundred years after the murder, reads:

WILLIAM TERRISS
1847 – 1897
HERO OF THE ADELPHI
MELODRAMAS
MET HIS UNTIMELY END
OUTSIDE THIS THEATRE
16 DEC 1897

The author

"Sis", he said faintly "Sis, I am stabbed." I put my arms round him to support him, when we both fell to the ground on the bare boards at the foot of the staircase leading to our dressing-rooms.

Medical help was quick to arrive, having been summoned from nearby Charing Cross Hospital. The Senior House Surgeon, a Mr Hayward, realised very quickly that the third blow was fatal, nothing could be done to save Terriss. He was too ill to be moved to his dressing-room. The end came a few moments before eight o'clock. Jessie Millward described his last moments:

He was lying on my right arm, and I held his hand in my left hand. We were now alone. He opened his eyes, and faintly squeezed my hand. "Sis! Sis!" He whispered. And that was all.

Terriss's son-in-law, Seymour Hicks was, at the time the stabbing took place, walking along Henrietta Street, which runs parallel to Maiden Lane, on his way to the Gaiety Theatre, where he was appearing in *The Circus Girl*. Being totally unaware of what had happened, he arrived at the theatre and made up for his part. On coming down to the stage, he was surprised to find his understudy dressed ready to go on in his place. The stage manager told him it would be impossible for him to appear as something terrible had happened.

Hicks recalled:

The first thought which flashed across my mind was that the news was of my wife, who at that time was lying very ill at Eastbourne, only just out of danger, and grief-stricken at the loss of our little baby boy, which had occurred a fortnight previously. I stood staring and speechless, waiting for the blow to fall which I knew would kill me. Seeing, I suppose, the terror in my eyes, for a minute no one spoke, and when at last I was able to summon up enough courage to say, "Well, tell me," I heard a voice through the noisy chorus of a comic song whisper, "Old man, Bill Terriss has been killed."

Hicks although profoundly shocked at the news and despite its gravity felt a sense of relief, that his beloved wife Ellaline was not the object of the evening's tragic events. He commented:

It may seem strange, but having lived a lifetime of agony in a terrible minute, so great was the relief to know that the one I loved most on earth was safe, that the only emotion I felt was one of great thankfulness, and though I trembled, no one about me guessed the real reason why.

Being the only relative close at hand that evening, he was firstly called upon to identify Prince. He could not recall ever having seen him before. Hicks described the scene:

I found myself in a small room facing a raving lunatic being held against the wall by two policemen. Had he been sane, so distraught was I, my first
impulse would have been to have taken his life, and this I am bound to say was in my mind as I hurried to the station, knowing, as I did, nothing of the circumstances. When however, I was within a few feet of a savage animal, for Prince, foaming at the mouth, looked little else, I became calm amidst the turmoil and commenced to think of all that was going on in a curiously detached way.

After visiting Bow Street Police Station, Hicks was taken to the

MISS ELLALINE TERRISS

Ellaline Terriss. Author's collection

Adelphi Theatre. Terriss's body had been carried up to his dressing-room. Fred Latham, the acting manager of the theatre accompanied Hicks to the dead actor's dressing-room. He left Hicks alone with his father-in-law's body. Hicks said he felt a great terror as the door was slowly opened:

> *Left alone, however, with all that was mortal of the man I had been so fond of, fear left me, for, as I knelt by the couch on which he lay, the calm on his face and the smile upon his lips seemed to bid me take a message to his loved ones not to grieve, for he was happy. In the serenity and quiet of that room I to this day feel sure I heard a voice say to me, "Are there men living such fools as to think there is no hereafter?" That night I knew beyond all shadow of doubt that William Terriss and myself would meet again.*

Seymour Hicks, Terriss's son-in-law.
Author's collection

Hick's dresser was sent to Terriss's house in Bedford Park, where Terriss's twenty-five-year-old actor son, Tom, had returned from rehearsals. He couldn't bring himself to tell the son of his father's death but brought him back to the Adelphi, where the news was broken to him.

The funeral took place five days later at Brompton Cemetery, being preceded by a service at the Chapel Royal of the Savoy. Terriss was laid to rest on the East Terrace, sharing a vault with his mother and his baby grandson who had been buried there two weeks previously. Terriss's wife did not attend the funeral. This was not unusual, as at that time close female relatives often did not attend funerals, which were essentially male occasions. Jessie Millward went in a carriage with Seymour Hicks and Sir Henry Irving. The official list of mourners included only two other women. *The Times* reported that some 50,000 people lined the streets to watch the funeral procession and pay their respects to their lost favourite of the London stage. Even the cemetery was crowded with people. The list of the great and the good, who sent flowers, was headed by the Prince of Wales. Eva Moore recalled in *Exits And Entrances*:

The murder scene. The Illustrated Police News

     ... *his funeral was a proof of the affection in which he was held – it was practically a "Royal" funeral. When, a few months ago, Marie Lloyd was buried, the crowds, the marks of affection, the very real and very deep regret shown everywhere, reminded me of another funeral – that of "Breezy Bill Terriss".*

Seymour Hicks wrote:

"Mr. A," the fellow-player who had been the indirect cause of his death, must, to do him justice, have suffered remorse beyond words, for James Beveridge and Charles Somerset, two of William Terriss's oldest comrades, years afterwards informed me of the terrible interview they had with him the day after the funeral, for when telling him that they lay their friend's death at his door he completely and utterly broke down.

Nothing was mentioned to the police about the affair and Abingdon was not called to give evidence at the trial. However, Prince's sister Maggie conveniently disappeared, sometime between the murder and the trial.

The inquest took place on the afternoon of Monday 20 December, at St Martin's Town Hall, before Mr John Troutbeck, coroner for Westminster. It was brief, as there was no doubt how Terriss had died and who had killed him. Witnesses having given their evidence and the coroner having summed up, the jury returned a verdict of wilful murder against Prince. The press had had a field day with such a sensational murder to write about. On Christmas Day, a more sober report was given in *The Illustrated Police News*:

For a very large section of the British public the gaiety of Christmastide has this year been sadly abated by the terrible end of the popular actor, Mr William Terriss, the hero of a hundred stage fights, who was stabbed to death on Thursday evening in last week outside the Adelphi Theatre.

The report goes on to describe the events of the evening and then goes on to say:

The tidings spread over London and thence throughout the kingdom like wild-fire, received everywhere first with incredulity and thence with indignant sorrow. To few even of fortune's favourites in the theatrical profession does it fall to be so closely in touch with the great heart of the playgoing public as the leading representative of British heroism had long been, and the dastardly nature of the crime, committed out of an unreasoning jealousy by a good-for-nothing, who had in the past received much kindness at his victim's hand, stirred the deep indignation even of those to whom the dead player's personality meant nothing.

The Illustrated London News also reported:

The Prisoner in the dock at Bow Street. The Illustrated Police News

In private life Mr. Terriss was as much beloved as by his friends of the playgoing public. Until the sudden outbreak of homicidal fury on the part of the man who now awaits trial for his dastardly act, it would have taxed the dead actor's friends to name the man who was his enemy. Sincere and generous, he led a simple, unaffected life, which in itself commanded respect, and was, in brief, one of whom –

... Nature might stand up
And say to all the world, "This was a man!"

Mr. Terriss leaves a widow, two sons, and a daughter. One of the sons has
given some promise as an actor, and the daughter Miss Ellaline Terriss
(Mrs. Seymour Hicks) is already known to fame as a comedienne of
exceptional charm.

In those days justice was far swifter than today. The trial took place
on 13 January 1898, less than a month after the murder and lasted
one day. It was an extremely disturbing affair. Prince was tried at the
Old Bailey before Mr Justice Channell. The prosecutor was Mr C F
Gill, assisted by Mr Horace Avory. Richard Archer Prince, swathed
in an Inverness cape was represented by Mr W H Sands. On 22
January 1898, *The Illustrated Police News* reported:

Immediately the prisoner took his seat at half-past ten he was called. He
entered the box with the same air of self-importance that he assumed
before the magistrate, and on the charge being read to him and the
question of guilty or not guilty asked, he answered in a clear voice,
"Guilty with provocation." Addressing the judge, he then claimed by the
law of England the right to be defended by a Queen's counsel. "I have
no friends of my own, and cannot pay a penny for my defence. If he must
be paid, those who drove me to it should pay." The judge pointed out that
this was not the law of the land, and advised him to be advised by his
counsel. Prince, after again exclaiming that he was guilty with the
greatest provocation, ultimately took the advice of the judge and
exclaimed, "I must say, then, not guilty."

John Henry Graves gave details of the actual killing. Three medical
experts from Holloway, the Doctors Bastian, Hyslop and Scott, gave
their opinions on Prince's mental state. Another medical expert,
Doctor Fitch, superintendent of a lunatic asylum in Salisbury,
explained the circumstances surrounding the death of James Archer,
Prince's half-brother, which served to highlight the mental instability
believed to have been inherent in that family. Prince's step-sister,
Maggie was absent from the trial. Referred to as 'Mrs Archer', she
was represented by a servant, Mary Waller. She testified that she

had heard that he was Mrs Archer's step-brother. He confirmed that he
had visited the house five or six times in November and December, but
not for a fortnight or so before the murder.

Other witnesses gave evidence concerning his theatrical and working background, and several family members, including his mother, brother and niece, as well as neighbours from Dundee, gave testimony to his strangeness. George Lauberg, who had sold Prince the knife with which he stabbed Terriss, was also a witness. The *Illustrated Police News* reported that the prisoner's mother in her evidence said:

> ... *her son was always peculiar, and when a child suffered from sunstroke. He often, when he grew up, complained of people blackmailing, and once said he was the Lord Jesus Christ and that she was the Virgin Mary. When he had his turns he would sing, be violent, write plays, and his eyes would stare out of his head. He said she poisoned his food.*

The same publication also reported:

> *Harry Archer said* [the] *prisoner, his brother, several times attacked him, and once used a knife and a poker. Witness went for the police at the time, but they took no steps because the prisoner had cooled down.*

All the evidence having been presented, Mr Justice Channell gave his summing up. *The Times* reported:

> *Having referred to the evidence and to the testimony of the medical experts, who had expressed the unanimous and undoubted opinion that the prisoner was insane, the learned Judge concluded by observing that the questions were, first, whether the jury were satisfied that the prisoner committed the act and, secondly, whether it had been made to appear to them that, at the time he committed it, he was not responsible, according to law, by reason of disease of the mind.*

The jury retired at 6.35 p.m., and having considered the evidence returned after just half an hour. They found Prince guilty of wilful murder, but taking the medical evidence into account, not responsible for his actions. The judge ordered that the prisoner be retained as a criminal lunatic at Holloway until Her Majesty's Pleasure be known. On hearing this Prince called out:

> *Shall I not be allowed to make a statement of thanks to the Court? I should like to thank all the gentlemen who have assisted in the case. I did*

The Last Act in the Adelphi Tragedy. The Illustrated Police News

not bring my defence properly forward after the medical evidence because I did not think it necessary, and because I should not have been believed. All that I can say is that I have had a very fair trial and that –

MR JUSTICE CHANNELL: *I cannot allow any statement now. It is better not.*

THE PRISONER: *All I can say is that I thank you.*
MR JUSTICE CHANNELL: *You are entitled to thank your counsel.*

Prince wished to continue but the judge had him removed from court.

Terriss's wife, Isabella who had not been well just before the murder, went with their son Tom to Algeria for a holiday. She did not live long after their return and died during the summer of 1898.

As for Terriss's leading lady and mistress, Jessie Millward, she suffered almost a total collapse after his death and vowed never to go on the stage again. However, with the support of her friends and after an extended holiday in Italy, she returned to the stage and almost a year after the murder opened at the Empire Theatre, New York, in *Phroso* an adaptation of the novel by Anthony Hope. She worked almost exclusively in America for the next fifteen years. In 1907, she married the Scottish actor John Glendinning. He had been working in America for over twenty years. Ironically, as a young actor he had appeared in tours of Adelphi Melodramas throughout the United Kingdom, often being billed as 'the Terriss of the North'. Jessie retired in 1913. Her husband died in 1916, at the age of fifty-eight. In 1923, she published her autobiography *Myself and Others,* a collaboration with the journalist J B Booth. She died in 1932.

Richard Archer Prince was not kept at the institution in Holloway for long, he was transferred to Broadmoor. Jessie Millward wrote of him in 1923:

Prince was, of course, found insane, and sent to Broadmoor Asylum for life. Some time later I heard he had been appointed to the position of gardener, and from Broadmoor he frequently wrote to actors at the Adelphi begging their influence to get him released and to secure him a part in the Adelphi play. At Broadmoor, for all I know, he still remains. Only recently did I hear of him, through the visit of an ex-Cabinet Minister to the asylum. In the visitor's honour a performance was given by the asylum band, the members of which were prisoners found insane. The conductor mounted to his desk, turned to the ex-Minister and gave him a majestic bow, then, tapping on his desk in manner of the professional chef d'orchestre, *proceeded to conduct the performance. That conductor was Prince, the murderer of my friend.*

Richard Archer Prince died at Broadmoor in 1937.

A dear friend of mine, the late actor, author and playwright, Richard Huggett, visited Broadmoor shortly before World War Two, as a boy, with his father, who was Professor of Physiology at St Mary's Hospital, Paddington. They saw a pantomime, which had been staged by the patients. He remembered a conversation, which at the time meant nothing to him. Several of the staff were heard to say, 'what a pity "Princey" wasn't here this year. How he would have enjoyed it'. Richard went on to research the events surrounding Terriss and Prince and his radio play *A Study in Hatred*, was aired on BBC Radio 4.

In so many autobiographies and accounts of the events surrounding the death of William Terriss which, including that of Jessie Millward (which totally ignores her true relationship with Terriss), glosses over the facts, including that it was generally known throughout the profession that Terriss's murderer had been egged on by Abingdon and others, with tragic consequences. Even as late as 1930, when Seymour Hicks published his *Between Ourselves*, he was still prepared to veil the identity of Abingdon. Although he described in some detail the cruel hoax which was played on Prince, he referred to him simply as 'Mr. A'. However in the penultimate paragraph of the chapter on The Murder of William Terriss, he states:

> *It was Fate which later took 'Mr. A' to America, where after appearing with some success for a considerable period, he too came to a tragic end. He was discovered dead, having committed suicide by cutting his throat.*

It did not take much to work out who 'Mr. A' was, even for those not in the know, particularly as Abingdon died by his own hand and by the method described by Hicks. Abingdon was found dead at his apartment at 235 West 76th Street, New York, on 19 May 1918.

The *Daily Telegraph* organised a Memorial Fund. A new Lifeboat House was built on the Grand Parade at Eastbourne, a place where Terriss had spent much of his leisure time. The inscription read:

> *This Life-boat House has been erected in memory of WILLIAM TERRISS with subscriptions received by the 'DAILY TELEGRAPH' from those who loved and admired him, and who sorrowed together with all his friends and fellow countrymen at his most untimely end.*

1898
"Shadows we are and shadows we pursue."

In Rotherhithe, a theatre which opened in 1899 was named the Terriss Theatre. It changed its name to the Rotherhithe Hippodrome in 1908.

The victim in this terrible tragedy, William Terriss, died at the height of his fame, still possessing the looks and physique of the romantic hero, and idolized by a vast and adoring public on both sides of the Atlantic. The saddest thing of all, is that today he is largely forgotten. Great and popular actor though he was, the melodramas which were the mainstay of his distinguished career, gave him little opportunity to stamp his mark on milestones of theatrical history. Nevertheless the man is a milestone himself, and both his gallantry as well as his contribution to the English speaking theatre should not be forgotten. Of Terriss, I leave the last words to one of our greatest actresses, Dame Ellen Terry, who said of her close colleague and intimate friend: 'He died a beautiful youth, a kind of Adonis, although he was fifty years old.'

The grave of William Terriss (second left), in Brompton Cemetery. The author

CHAPTER 12

The Strange Disappearance of Victor Grayson
1920

*'But you say at the same time that you are convinced
he is dead. Why?' I inquired.
'I am certain he was murdered,' replied Ryan.*

Victor Grayson occupied the political stage for less than a decade. He served as a Member of Parliament for just two and a half years. In 1907, when he was twenty-five, his sensational bi-election victory as a Socialist (according to Reg Groves, one of Grayson's biographers, the only Socialist ever to be elected to the House of Commons), made all the more dramatic because the Labour Party, then in its infancy, had refused to adopt him as their candidate, seemed to herald a brilliant political career. In the General Election of 1910, he lost his seat but he had caught the imagination of a discontented electorate across the entire country. Before he had the opportunity to appear on the parliamentary stage again, the Great War intervened and towards the end of it, he suffered the tragic loss of his wife in childbirth. Disoriented, disillusioned and increasingly over indulgent in alcoholic stimulation, he began to mix with men of a different political persuasion to his own, including Horatio Bottomley (the swindler) and the honours tout Maundy Gregory. He got a bee in his bonnet about what he considered to be an abuse of the honours system, and following his investigations and some sensational claims of political impropriety, namely regarding the actual sale of honours, he threatened to spill the beans. Then in 1920, he disappeared completely, and it wasn't until seven years elapsed that the general public at large were even aware of the fact. Had these strange new associations for a Socialist, anything to do with his disappearance? The last official sighting of Grayson was in the heart of the West End. Although there were many reported so-called sightings of him until at least the nineteen forties, none were fully corroborated. Foul play has been at the heart of the many theories that surround

Grayson's disappearance. The story of his known existence is an intriguing one.

Named Albert Victor, after the Duke of Clarence, the eldest son of the then Prince of Wales, later Edward VII, Victor Grayson was born in Liverpool on 5 September 1881 (a seventh son). In the six weeks between his birth and registration the family had moved from 8 Talieson Street to 15 Elstow Street in the Kirkdale district. His mother, Elizabeth Craig, was a native of Scotland, who had been brought up in the Highlands. After her parents died she moved to Ireland where she went into domestic service. There she met and fell in love with a young soldier from Yorkshire. His name was William Dickenson. According to family legend he deserted and took her away with him by ship to Liverpool, married her and they settled there. He changed his name to Grayson to avoid detection. William was a devout Christian, who had a thorough knowledge of the bible. He found work as a carpenter and settled down to married life.

Victor Grayson received his elementary education at St Matthew's Church of England School in Liverpool's infamous Scotland Road. From an early age he was an avid reader, cutting his teeth on penny dreadfuls and the like. Victor spent the early years of his life growing up in a typical working-class district, a district more aptly described as that of skilled artisans' dwellings than of slums. After he left school, the family moved home several times, and following his father's death, finally settled at 137 Northcote Street where his mother died in 1929, reportedly grieving the disappearance of her famous son. On leaving school he spent six years as an apprentice turner at the Bankhall Engine Works of J H Wilson. At the age of

eighteen he began attending Bethel Mission in Edinburgh Street. He gained experience as a public speaker, firstly as a Sunday School teacher, and later by addressing outdoor Christian meetings. After two years he decided to move on as he disagreed with some of the teachings at the Bethel Mission. Instead he went to the Hamilton Road Mission, where he made contact with the pastor of the Anfield Unitarian Church, the Revd J L Haigh, who

Victor Grayson, during the bi-election campaign of 1907.
Author's collection

recognized that young Victor possessed considerable talents and took him under his wing.

The Reverend Haigh became Victor's mentor and such was Haigh's influence that Victor decided to follow him into the Unitarian Church. While he continued working as an engineer, he assisted at the Mission in the evenings and at weekends. He took the Sunday School and became an active participant in the Mission's debating society, which gave him scope to develop his talents as a speaker. He took on board the things he heard and refashioned them in his own way, becoming, according to Reg Groves, without being aware of it, a socialist, and it was as a socialist that he expressed his views. With the Reverend Haigh's help, Grayson got into Liverpool University, then in the autumn of 1904 he went to Owen's College, Manchester to study for the ministry. The College specialized in training recruits from industrial areas for the Unitarian Church, and undertook financial responsibility for poorer students, providing the opportunity for bright young men from working-class backgrounds to enter the ministry.

Not only were the closing years of Queen Victoria's reign Victor Grayson's formative years, they were also the formative years of the labour movement. Two forces were being galvanized into action, the forces of socialism and the forces of trade unionism. The Independent Labour Party was founded in 1893 from several Yorkshire and Lancashire socialist societies, including the Colne Valley Labour League (later to become Colne Valley Socialist League).

Grayson's interest in politics was gathering momentum and by 1905 he spent an increasing amount of time on Socialist politics at the expense of his studies. He addressed many meetings in various Lancashire towns but it was to be across the border in Yorkshire, that a great opportunity came his way and set him on the path to Westminster. In December 1905 during the course of the General Election campaign, in Huddersfield, a prominent trade union leader, Will Thorne, was booked to address a meeting at the Town Hall on 16 December, in support of the Labour candidate, T Russell Williams. Thorne was unable to attend and Grayson was invited to stand in for him. He gave a dazzling performance. His speech electrified the audience who were mesmerized by the powerful oratory of this relatively unknown young man. Grayson presented his political views like an evangelist presents his love of God; in an age when England abounded with great political orators, Grayson excelled. Both friends and foe alike agreed that he was phenomenal on the platform. He seldom used notes and possessed that rare gift that enabled him to marshall his thoughts into logical sentences whilst on his feet. He possessed a natural wit and repartee, which allowed him to turn the mood of any crowd and to extricate himself from any difficulties he might encounter with hecklers. He did not speak in any particular dialect, and those who passed any comment on his speaking voice regarding any trace of accent, described it as 'faintly northern'.

That speech in Huddersfield, on 16 December 1905, established Victor Grayson as a serious politician, in the eyes of the district's socialists and he became an overnight celebrity. Grayson made a particular impression on the members of the Colne Valley Labour League. Many invitations followed and the young, debonair, good looking theology student found himself addressing meetings across the straggling Colne Valley constituency, which stretched to within ten miles of Manchester. By July 1906 Grayson decided that despite his deep religious convictions, life as a minister was not for him and he was given permission by the College authorities to withdraw from his course.

In Colne Valley rumours were spreading that the local Liberal MP, Sir James Kitson, was to be elevated to the House of Lords; this would mean a by-election. When Kitson became Lord Airedale in mid June 1907, the Colne Valley Labour League had already made its contingency plans and Victor Grayson was officially adopted as their candidate on 22 June 1907. The Labour Party's national body was composed of representatives of trade unions, the Fabian Society and the ILP (Independent Labour Party, a body committed to democratic socialism). There had been some trouble about Grayson's candidature. The national leaders of the ILP did not favour the choice made locally in Colne valley, they had their own choice of candidates in mind, namely Bruce Glasier and W C Anderson. There were some who thought that the twenty-five-year-old Grayson was too young. In those days Members of Parliament were not paid, support was usually provided from Labour Party and Independent Labour Party funds. Despite this the Colne Valley Labour League stood their ground and Grayson fought the election as a socialist, and was not officially adopted by the Labour Party, as both the party and the ILP refused either to support or endorse him.

The by-election took place on Thursday 18 July and Grayson won the seat at the expense of the Liberals. It was a close run contest, of the 11,671 voters on the Electoral Roll, 10,370 voted, a turnout of 88%, the result being:

Albert **Victor** Grayson (Socialist) 3,648
Philip Bright (Liberal) 3,495
J C H Wheeler (Conservative) 3,227

Victor Grayson went to take his seat in the House of Commons with very little money of his own. It was not until the Independent Labour Party met on 25 August that they agreed to pay Grayson a Parliamentary allowance of £220 until their annual conference at Easter 1908. This was the amount the Labour Party paid its MPs, and in return they expected Grayson to accept conference decisions, as he was in receipt of their money. Grayson might have been a great orator but his performance as an MP was not so impressive, his inactivity on the Parliamentary scene did not escape the attention of his political opponents, nor the newspapers:

In 1907 of the possible 149 divisions, he voted in 21 (14%)
In 1908 of the possible 463 divisions, he voted in 33 (7%)
In 1909 of the possible 920 divisions, he voted in 51 (5.5%)

As far as speeches and debates were concerned, Grayson did not use his skills to any great effect in the house:

In 1907 he made 1 speech and asked 3 questions
In 1908 he made 1 speech, asked 5 questions and made 2 interventions
In 1909 he made 1 speech and made 1 intervention

In his book *The Problem of Parliament,* published during his time as an MP, in 1909, in conjunction with G R S Taylor, Grayson wrote:

We have examined the history and achievements of the Whig Party, the Tory Party, the Trade Unionists, and, finally, the Labour Party. It is not a matter of speculation, but a sad historical fact, that as instruments of Reform they have all been the most dismal of failures. No one would maintain that they have not seen, during their time, many beneficial changes which have a certain right to be ascribed to their influence and energy. It is rather a surface credit, after all said and done. Nature has a way of shuffling on its career towards something better, and goes this way without depending very seriously on the help of the politicians, whether they be Radicals or Conservatives or Labour men or Socialists. No Government has yet had the audacity to sit on the Wheels of Destiny, which insist on going round for the sheer love of the thing. But, on the other hand, no Government or Party or Association which has reached the political stage in any coherent form, has the courage to offer its aid to Dame Nature.

Since he became an MP, Grayson had become increasingly friendly with the editor of the *Clarion*, Robert Blatchford and in February 1909, Blatchford offered Grayson a job on the paper. This provided Grayson with the opportunity to reach a wide readership and he accepted the offer. The relationship between Blatchford and Grayson grew closer, with the result that Grayson's actions both inside and outside the House of Commons were steadfastly defended in the columns of the *Clarion*. However, Grayson was becoming very sloppy with the way he organized his meetings, at which he would take to the platform and mesmerize the audience with his oratory skills. He would sometimes book two, or even three, to take place within a single day, the result being that he was unable to get to them all, and this led to a certain amount of ill will. Despite this carelessness, within the Colne Valley itself, his popularity remained undiminished. When he addressed open air gatherings, crowds of working men and women would follow him from meeting to meeting. However, within the Colne Valley Socialist League, there was dissention in the ranks, prompted by the League's president, Francis Littlewood, a close friend of Philip Snowden, who had opposed Grayson's candidature in the first place. In the General Election of January 1910, Grayson lost his Colne Valley seat, being beaten into third place, the result was:

Dr Charles Leach (Liberal)	4,741
A Boyd Carpenter (Conservative)	3,750
Victor Grayson (Socialist)	3,149

After two and a half years with a controversial MP, creating one incident after another, the electorate made their opinions very clear and the Liberals won handsomely. After losing his seat, Grayson continued to work as political editor on the *Clarion*, which had some years previously moved its main office from Manchester to London. In December 1908, he stood as a Socialist in the bi-election in Kennington. However, his candidature was not decided until ten days before polling, and his campaign scarcely had time to gather momentum. He did not fare well. The Liberals hung on to their seat, but only just, with a majority of fifty-five over the Tories. The result was:

S Collins (Liberal)	3,565
F A Lucas (Conservative)	3,510
Victor Grayson (Socialist)	408

Since moving to London Grayson had struck up a friendship with the actor-manager Arthur Rose, a committed Socialist. Rose introduced the former MP to actresses. It was said that Victor Grayson's good looks and engaging personality made him very attractive to the opposite sex. Reg Groves recorded an interview with Rose:

Between Victor and me there existed the kind of affection that can grow up between two men ... a love deeper, perhaps, than the love between man and woman. Victor's marriage did him credit, mind. You see we had both said we would never marry. Victor felt, as I did, that we ought to be free to devote all our time to the cause ... I knew a great deal about Victor's many relationships with women. You can't blame Victor. He attracted women; he was, well, like a matinee idol. He had the loveliest women in the movement – and outside it, too – throwing themselves at him. He was only human. Which one of us can be sure we'd behave differently in similar circumstances?

It is clear from his letters and some of his associations that Victor had homosexual leanings. It is known that he carried on a relationship with his Merseyside friend, Harry Dawson. It appears he enjoyed a bisexual lifestyle and during the latter part of his known existence, following the death of his wife, largely preferred the company of men. He did like to be seen in female company from time to time and following his wife's death he often escorted Hilda Porter, manageress of his London apartment block, to the theatre. His good friend Robert Blatchford, whose daughter, Win, was attracted to Grayson, was not at all keen on her becoming romantically attached to him, as he was aware of Grayson's proclivities, and wrote in a letter of Victor:

I have never seen him show nor heard him express any regard for any woman. His general attitude towards the whole sex is one of suspicion. I have never known a young man so cold towards women. I don't think he ever loved anybody. There is always something odd about him. I don't think he will ever marry and I don't think he or his wife would be at all happy if he did.

However, much to the surprise of many who knew him, during the first week of November 1912, Victor married a twenty-five-year-old actress, who worked under the name of Ruth Norreys (Ruth Nightingale was her actual name and she was the daughter of John Nightingale, of Bolton, in Lancashire, General Manager of the County Bank, Manchester), at Chelsea Registry Office. They were to live in Stockwell Park Road. Married life with Grayson could not have been easy. To his wife's credit she stayed loyal to him through periods of extreme depravation, she nursed him in illness, shared his political platforms and even became the family breadwinner. He suffered a bout of illness in November 1912 and the following February had a more serious nervous breakdown. Following the intervention of his friends, including Arthur Rose, a letter was published in the *Clarion,* stating that he was to take a rest, ideally involving a long sea voyage. They launched a national appeal to raise funds to enable him to take this necessary recuperation. Within three months, £106 16*s* 10*d* had been subscribed from supporters all over Britain. Financial considerations had meant that Victor and Ruth had moved from Stockwell Park Road to Theobald Street. A young journalist, Fenner Brockway, visited them there. He commented in an interview some seventy years later:

> *I have rarely seen anyone in such utter poverty as they were. They were living in one room, slept on the floor. It's the only time I've seen a sugar-box used as a table.*

The appeal enabled Victor and Ruth to travel, firstly to Italy and after five weeks there, they took a long sea voyage to New York. In his absence bankruptcy proceedings had been instigated and a petition had been filed against him on 26 August 1913, with a receiving order made against him on 9 January 1914. On his return to England, Victor gave an interview which appeared in the *Huddersfield Examiner* on 14 January 1914, in which he made no reference to his financial struggles but made various comparisons between life in America and in England. The purpose of the interview was to promote a political come-back. The first meeting of his creditors took place on 26 January. They decided to give him some time to see if he could raise capital. He owed £496, against assets of just £1. At the next meeting exactly a month later, he had managed to raise sufficient capital and the majority of his creditors accepted his terms. The court approved his offer to pay 7*s* 6*d* in the pound, in addition to paying costs. Grayson narrowly escaped bankruptcy, which would have prevented him entering the House of Commons again. A daughter, Elaine, was born on 13 April 1914 and following the birth the family lived at 15

Manor Gardens, Larkhall Rise, Clapham, for the next year. By the beginning of 1914, Victor had resigned himself to the fact that he had been rejected by the party he had so long supported, his pro-war stance alienated him from the rank and file of the party and this meant that he would soon split with the *Clarion* group. He wasn't getting as many invitations to speak and with the coming of the war and with little hope of support in the forthcoming election, he finally withdrew his candidature from Colne Valley on 21 April 1915.

The war had prompted Grayson to rethink many of his previous opinions. In the London *Evening Standard* on 20 January 1915, he wrote:

> *The other day I came across a list of Lords who were serving at the front ... Looking at the figures dispassionately, I think that our titled persons have given a good account of themselves. Our old point of view was that nobody with anything material to lose would enter the game of warfare. That old point of view must be abandoned ... One hundred and seventy-eight peers are fighting at the front. The soil of France is already covered with their blue blood. They are fighting and dying for what they call Liberty ...*

Could Grayson's change in attitude, both during and immediately following the Great War have had anything to do with a discovery made on his part? Victor Grayson was said to have possessed a natural aristocratic bearing, he had an air of elegance, liked fine clothes, good whisky, wine and foods, and it was said of him that money simply 'dribbled through his fingers'. There is certainly some evidence which might suggest that he was the illegitimate son of an aristocrat and it has been suggested that in the intervening six weeks between his birth and the removal of the family from Talieson Street to Elstow Street in the Kirkdale district of Liverpool, might have been to distract attention from a new arrival in the household, an arrival which could not be easily explained at the old address. Further weight was added to this theory when Georgina Nightingale, Grayson's mother-in-law, was dying; Grayson's daughter, Elaine, and the family maidservant, Jane, were in attendance. Towards the end of what had been a constant vigil of several days, the old lady took her granddaughter's hand and kept repeating the name 'the Marlboroughs'. Following her grandmother's funeral, Elaine mentioned her grandmother's utterings, and Jane, who had been in the Nightingales' service for many years, in fact for all her working life, said, 'Elaine, didn't you realize your grandmother was telling you who your father really was?' Some have likened Grayson's appearance to Winston Churchill, whose father, Lord Randolph Churchill, was the son of the Duke of Marlborough, another indication, it has been said, that Grayson's parentage was not as the official version would have it.

In the Spring of 1915, Ruth obtained an engagement with the Allan Wilkie Shakespearean Company for a tour of the Antipodes and Victor decided to accompany her. In Australia there was considerable demand for Victor to speak at public meetings. The great orator was in his element, and the fees he earned were a boost to the family's finances. After touring Australia, the theatrical company set sail for New Zealand and Victor went with them. They docked in Auckland on 5 April 1916. His reputation as a former Socialist MP preceded him and he was booked for a series of lectures in three centres, for an agreed fee of £50. He gave his final lecture on 13 November before he enlisted (as a result of being goaded at several meetings for not having the courage of his convictions, by participating in the conflict himself) in the Expeditionary Forces on 28 November, as 45001 Private Victor Grayson. While Ruth continued to play the Nurse in *Romeo and Juliet,* Victor knuckled down to army life. Ruth and her daughter, Elaine, arrived back in England on 23 June 1917. Victor was posted to C Company 25th Reinforcements and disembarked at Davenport on 20 July 1917, after a long sea voyage. On 5 September he left for France. On 19 October 1917 the Press Association reported that:

> *Private Victor Grayson, ex-M.P. for Colne Valley, was wounded during last Friday's offensive and is now in hospital in France.*

Victor had received a shrapnel wound in the hip and was suffering from a nervous disorder. While he received treatment, Ruth and Elaine were in Bolton, staying with the Nightingales, enjoying the home comforts that their upper-middle-class home allowed. On 15 December, Victor appeared before the medical board at Brockenhurst, and was subsequently discharged from the army as physically unfit. The board recommended that he be awarded a thirty per cent disability pension for six months, which he never claimed. Just before Christmas 1917, Victor was granted leave and given orders to report to the discharge depot at Torquay on 3 January. He didn't receive his discharge until 7 March. Meanwhile, a tragedy had intervened. On 6 February 1918 Ruth Grayson gave birth prematurely to a daughter, Elsie, who lived for only fifteen minutes. Four days later, on 10 February, Ruth herself died from the after-effects of childbirth, in a nursing home at 42, Belgrave Road, London, which could only have served to aggravate Victor's nervous disorder. It is not known when Ruth became a Catholic convert. Victor certainly did not follow her. She was buried in St Mary's Catholic Cemetery, Kensal Green. The gravestone was expensively fashioned from granite and was paid for by her father. The inscription reads:

TO THE SWEET MEMORY OF
RUTH GRAYSON
(RUTH NORREYS)
DEARLY LOVED AND ONLY CHILD OF
JOHN W. & GEORGINA NIGHTINGALE
BORN MARCH 11TH 1887
DIED FEBRUARY 10TH 1918
"Eternal rest give unto her O Lord
and let perpetual light shine upon her."

"REQUIESCAT IN PACE"

It is puzzling why there was no mention of her husband on the inscription Ruth left £48 2s 0d and letters of administration were

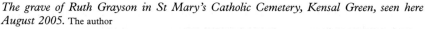

The grave of Ruth Grayson in St Mary's Catholic Cemetery, Kensal Green, seen here August 2005. The author

granted to her father on 11 May. Perhaps Grayson's mental state at the time was too fragile to enable him to cope with his late wife's affairs. His mother said:

The shock of his wife's death was a very great blow to him. So, too, was the death of his brother, Jack, who was killed in France while serving with the Grenadier Guards. He was deeply in love with Ruth and she with him.

Grayson's star was soon on the rise again. He earned some income from contributions to various journalistic publications and once again assumed the mantle of the great orator, making speeches at political meetings. In *The Strange Case of Victor Grayson,* Reg Groves writes of one particular speech:

At a public meeting in Liverpool that year [1919] *he demanded 'a searching, independent investigation of the whole question of selling titles' and went on to say:*

'Our sailors and soldiers, who have fought so gallantly to throw off the tyranny of the German junkers, are promised by the Prime Minister that they will have a land fit for heroes to live in.

What do they get? A miserable pittance on which to start life anew, the permanent threat of unemployment and never a word of credit. What do they see? The war profiteers with so much money that they pay tens of thousands for a barony. I declare that this sale of honours is a national scandal. It can be traced right down from Number Ten Downing Street, to a monocled dandy with offices in Whitehall, who organizes the greatest piece of chicanery this country has known since the days of the Rotten Boroughs. I know this man and one day I will name him.'

These were very dangerous assertions which some feel may well have been at the crux of Grayson's disappearance. He was pointing his finger directly at Maundy Gregory. Gregory might well have felt threatened by Grayson. He had acquired a palatial office at 38 Parliament Street, Westminster, from which he operated his brokerage services. Between 1916 and 1923, Lloyd George nominated ninety-one new peers – twice the average. Many nominees were highly questionable candidates to be the recipients of such high honours and it was noted in some quarters that several war profiteers were included. Broadly speaking the tariff for honours ranged from £10,000 for a knighthood, £30,000 for a baronetcy and between £50,000 and £100,000 for a peerage. Gregory received his substantial 'commission' and Lloyd George's party coffers were swelled by considerable amounts into the bargain. Gregory was eventually brought to account in part in 1933, when he served two months in prison plus a fine of £50 and costs for certain improprieties under the new Honours Act but had the matter come to light when his operation was at its height, the whole affair would have been a very serious matter indeed, and extremely embarrassing for many in the highest echelons of society.

So we now come to September 1920, when Victor Grayson mysteriously disappeared. The last time Grayson saw his mother was at her Liverpool home and following his final departure from Northbrook Street, her final residence, the evidence about his subsequent movements is conflicting and confusing. Some say he was due to address a meeting in Hull, while others deny the existence of any such meeting. From reports of the events that followed, it seems fairly certain that he caught a train to London from Liverpool. Weeks went by, then months. His friends and relatives were not surprised at hearing no news from him, because they were accustomed to Victor's periodic disappearances. The general public simply assumed he had withdrawn from public life. Although his mother was worried about her son's disappearance, she was not unduly alarmed, but as months turned into years, she had almost given up hope of ever seeing Victor alive again. On 20 March 1927 the *World's Pictorial News* included an article about Grayson's disappearance seven years previously. The article included statements made by his mother, in which she said:

If Victor is alive – which I strongly doubt – he must be wandering about suffering from loss of memory.

It transpired that early in September 1920, Grayson had told a friend, Mr E K Donovan, that he had reason to believe that he had enemies and that 'someone wants to do me an injury'.

Georgian House, Bury Street, SW1, seen from Ryder Street in August 2005, where Victor Grayson rented a flat on the fourth floor. The author

Donovan recalled that Grayson told him that he had been attacked and beaten up somewhere near the Strand. According to his family, Grayson told them that the injuries he had sustained had been as a result of a fall. He had a broken arm and a head wound which required stitches. Although the records for that period from the Charing Cross Hospital are missing, the last important piece of information the Metropolitan Police had of Grayson was of an attack on him somewhere near the Strand.

According to most reliable reports concerning the last confirmed sighting of Grayson, several stated that he went to London. Most, but not all, of them say that he stayed in the *Georgian Hotel*. However, in *Kelly's Directory* for 1920, there is no such place listed as the *Georgian Hotel*. The directory does list the Georgian Restaurant at 43 Chandos Place, which features in the last known days of Victor Grayson. The building still exists but the Georgian Restaurant has been closed for decades. However, most importantly, David Clark in *Victor Grayson Labour's Lost Leader,* mentions that from late in 1918, Grayson rented an apartment near St James's Palace, in a prestigious block, called, surprisingly enough, Georgian House, situated at 10 Bury Street, SW1, for the very large sum of five guineas a week. His apartment, suite forty-two, was on the fourth floor. The manageress of the apartment block, Hilda Porter, came to know Grayson very well. She said he spent a great deal of his time sitting at his desk, writing. He had a regular set of gentlemen callers, principally, Robert Blatchford, the Socialist pamphleteer and journalist, Joseph Havelock Wilson, leader of the Seamen's Union, Horatio Bottomley, Liberal MP for South Hackney (found guilty of twenty-three counts of fraud, in 1923 and sentenced to seven years' imprisonment) and Maundy Gregory (failed actor and impresario, private detective, MI5 informer, would-be blackmailer, publisher of the *Whitehall Gazette* and honours tout).

Some accounts say that following his last visit to his mother, saying he would be in touch again the following day, Grayson caught the train to London where he joined some New Zealand officers for drinks in the bar of the Georgian Restaurant. What seems to be generally agreed, in most accounts surrounding Grayson's disappearance, is that one September evening in 1920, he walked into the bar of the Georgian Restaurant, met some friends and ordered whiskies. At about six o'clock, after putting his half-empty glass down and picking up his walking stick, he said:

Don't let anyone drink my whisky. I shall be back in a few minutes.

Then he walked out into Chandos Place and into the Strand. He didn't return to finish his drink and he was never seen again. Donald McCormick claims that while Grayson was at the Georgian Restaurant, a message came for him, telling him that his luggage had been delivered in error to the *Queen's Hotel*, Leicester Square. David Clark comments that he thinks it odd that Grayson's luggage should have been delivered anywhere in London, other than to his apartment. Clark writes:

> *It is Hilda Porter who is able to provide us with the last substantiated sighting of Victor Grayson. She recalls that one mid-morning in late September 1920 – she does not remember the precise date and of course had no reason to do so – two strangers came and asked for Grayson. They sent up a visiting card and he invited them to his rooms. They stayed there most of the day, sending out for some drinks. Towards evening, the two men descended in the rickety lift and called a taxi. A few minutes later, Victor appeared carrying two very large suitcases. When he came out of the lift, he put down the cases, ascended the few stairs and went to the manageress's office. He told her, "I am having to go away for a while. I'll be in touch shortly." With these few words he rejoined the two men and went out to the taxi. That was the last she saw of Victor Grayson. The departure worried Hilda Porter, so after a while she inquired of the hall porter if he knew who the two men were but he had never seen them before. Half-an-hour or so later she went up to Grayson's room only to find all his personal effects missing – he had obviously taken them. Hoping against hope that he would return, she kept his rooms vacant for some time, but she was never to hear from him again.*

Bury Street, St James's, Victor Grayson's last known place of residence, seen here August 2005. Georgian House, where Grayson had a luxury suite, is above and to the left of the Tryon Gallery. Author's collection

Hilda Porter could not remember Grayson having received any injuries. His sister said:

> *We know that he left the hotel in which he was staying and never returned for his clothes. When I went to the hotel to see him the manageress told me Victor had taken his stick from the stand saying that he was going for a short walk. He was seen later with two Anzac officers, drinking in a nearby hotel. He left with two men and was never seen again.*

In newspaper reports and other accounts of the last known hours of Victor Grayson there are various inconsistencies. Some mention two hotels, one in which he was staying, the other, the *Georgian*, in which he was on the evening he was last seen. However, the name of the actual hotel in which he was supposedly staying was never mentioned by name. There is however, some significance in the *Queen's Hotel*, Leicester Square, where his luggage was taken by mistake, tenuous though the link is. It was this very hotel that Maundy Gregory used during the Great War, during his days in counter-espionage.

A more recent report of Grayson's supposed last drink was in a letter published in the *Daily Mirror* 3 March 1967, written by Miss Vicky Scrivener, of Watling Gardens, London NW2. She wrote:

> *I was intrigued to read about the Victor Grayson mystery in* Live Letters *because, you see, our family believes that one of our relatives was connected with the M.P.'s disappearance. At the time Grayson vanished people who were in the hotel with him claimed that a mysteriously veiled woman put her head round the door and beckoned to him. Grayson went out to her and was never seen again. My father told me that this mysterious woman was thought to be his aunt, a Suffragette who was friendly with Grayson. She vanished about the same time, never to be heard of again.*

In the 1921 annual report of the *Unitarian Magazine*, published from

The site of the Georgian Restaurant, at 43 Chandos Place, seen here in August 2005. The author

Owen's College, Grayson's name was given as being among those old students who had died that year. However, no reason for this statement was given by the college authorities.

Donald McCormick states in *Murder by Perfection* published in 1970:

> *Information about Victor Grayson in 1919 and 1920 is not easy to come by. Most of the people who knew him are dead, the few who still remember the debonair orator are somewhat hazy in their recollections about events of so long ago. Occasionally during this period there were brief references in the newspapers to Victor Grayson, but rarely more than an odd paragraph or two. The truth was that he had faded from the political scene; he talked of making a comeback, but it never amounted to much more than talk.*

One man was adamant that he saw Grayson on the afternoon of Tuesday 28 September 1920, and if true it may well have been after his 'disappearance' from the West End. The man in question was an English painter domiciled in Switzerland and Grayson had actually stayed with him during 1919, and sat for him as a model for a portrait. So presumably he was more than familiar with Grayson's appearance. George Flemwell was a painter, naturalist and writer. He came to England for a short stay in 1920 and it was he, who, while painting watercolours, on the Middlesex bank of the River Thames, close to Hampton Court Palace insisted that he saw Victor Grayson. Flemwell said he saw a motorized canoe, sailing quite close to the Middlesex bank. This type of vessel was something of a novelty at that time. There were two men in it and he recognized one as Victor Grayson. Too late to call out as the canoe sped by, Flemwell saw the canoe veer off to Ditton Island and he watched as it stopped at the jetty outside a bungalow and the two men got out and went inside. Anxious to see his friend before he returned to Switzerland, Flemwell was rowed across to the island by a ferryman, and he knocked on the door of the bungalow. The woman who answered the door was quite agitated and angrily denied any knowledge of Grayson. Flemwell was pretty nonplussed by this and within a few days returned to Switzerland. It later transpired that the bungalow in question, *Vanity Fair*, belonged to Maundy Gregory and it was also occupied by his housekeeper, Mrs Edith Rosse, a former actress. Gregory did indeed own a motorized canoe and at that time it was the only one in the area.

One theory that has been expounded by biographers and commentators alike, on the disappearance of Victor Grayson, is the likelihood of him having being murdered by, or on the instructions of, Maundy Gregory. Some wonder if he was lured to *Vanity Fair*, Gregory's waterside bungalow, then killed and his body disposed of in a watery grave and never discovered. Further weight has been added to this when Gregory was suspected of having murdered his housekeeper, Edith Rosse. The theory being that she knew what had happened to Grayson and she was disposed of when she threatened to reveal all.

There have been many theories expounded by biographers and journalists alike as the likeliest reason for Grayson's disappearance. There are four principal theories. The first is that Grayson was murdered, and his body hidden away and never discovered. The second, is that he committed suicide. He was certainly subject to bouts of depression and he had been hitting the bottle rather heavily. However, this possibility seems unlikely, as with suicides there is usually a body. The third theory is that he decided to make a clean break from his old life and to take on a new identity. He had told his sister that if ever he disappeared the family were not to worry about him, and that he would get in touch with them under a pen-name. It has been suggested that he might have cemented a relationship with a society lady, who made it a condition that he change his name and sever his links with the past. He never got in touch with his family again, there never were any letters from Victor, using a pen-name. The fourth theory, one that his mother referred to in 1927, is that he suffered a complete loss of memory and never recovered it.

Despite many searches, including those made by Scotland Yard, Victor Grayson's disappearance remains a mystery.

In December 1920 the New Zealand authorities sent a letter to Grayson to his last known address, asking him to attend a medical examination but they did not receive a reply. He never claimed the disability allowance he was entitled to.

Other accounts concerning Grayson's disappearance and/or whereabouts after 1920 include:

That he was alive in Ireland and had joined the IRA. It is known that Grayson did make several journeys to Ireland. Donald McCormick writes in *Murder by Perfection*:

Way back in 1936 I had an interview in Dublin with Frank Ryan, a former I.R.A. leader … In the course of conversation with him the name Victor Grayson was mentioned. At the time interest in Grayson had been revived because of various reports that he had been seen alive, Ireland being one of the countries named as his place of residence.

"I am quite certain that Grayson is not in Ireland and that he is dead," declared Ryan emphatically.

"Why are you so sure?" I asked.

"First of all," replied Ryan, "because I knew Grayson. It is true he visited Ireland after the war more than once, but he never once suggested that he wanted to live here, or that he wished to join the Party, as we called it then. He couldn't have joined us even if he had wished. God bless him, we loved Victor Grayson, but he was a crusader, not a revolutionary. No, Grayson was more interested in gathering evidence against what the British had being doing in Ireland than in wanting to join our cause. He was for us, but not of us, if you follow my meaning."

"But you say at the same time that you are convinced he is dead. Why?" I inquired.

"I am certain he was murdered," replied Ryan.

It was claimed that Grayson attended a Labour Party Meeting in Maidstone in 1924. The Labour candidate for Maidstone, Seymour Cocks said, 'on 23 August 1924, when I was addressing a meeting in the constituency, a man introduced himself as Victor Grayson and said he had been to New Zealand. He gave a Belfast address which since I have lost.' However, Mr Cocks did not make this matter known until 11 March 1927, when articles appeared in the press about Grayson having disappeared towards the end of 1920.

Ernest Marklew, who had been elected Labour MP for Colne Valley in 1935, and who had been active during the by-election of 1907, revealed that he had discovered the whereabouts of Victor Grayson. Shortly before his death in 1939, Marklew told veteran Huddersfield Socialist, Jess Townsend, that he had traced Grayson to a furniture shop in London, which he apparently owned. He said Grayson had begged him not to publicize the details as he had turned his back on public life. The thought of the sophisticated Grayson running a furniture shop is difficult to swallow.

In 1939, Sidney Campion, a one-time Independent Labour Party member, who had met Grayson on several occasions, was working in the Parliamentary Press Gallery for Kemsley Newspapers. In June 1939 he was travelling on the District Line from his home in Wimbledon to his work at the House of Commons. At Sloane Square station a smartly dressed couple boarded the train. He immediately recognized the man as Victor Grayson. Campion said that Grayson looked very prosperous and was wearing morning dress and a top hat. Campion says he was reluctant to approach Grayson and later regretted this. His vivacious female companion, who Campion said looked about twenty years younger than Grayson, was exquisitely dressed. As the couple chatted, the woman at one point referred to her companion as 'Vic'. As the train pulled into Westminster station, Campion says the man he believed to be Grayson turned to the woman and said, 'Here's the old firm', and the woman said that he must take her in some time. Campion told his colleagues about this sighting and there was some press coverage about the supposed sighting. Campion later claimed that he knew from a 'reliable' source, what had happened to Grayson. Refusing to reveal his source, he claimed that Grayson had become disenchanted by Socialism and had converted to the Conservative cause. He had offered his services to the party's then leader, Andrew Bonar Law, who had accepted his terms and agreed to help create a new identity and start a new life. He met an attractive woman who helped him in his career in the City. According to Campion, Grayson died in 1941, in an air raid in Chelsea. In 1940, Campion left journalism, after he was invited to become Public Relations Officer at the GPO, a position he did not apply for but the position was offered to him by the Prime Minister, Winston Churchill. This strange intervention in securing this relatively unimportant post in a time of war, by Churchill himself, seems to throw further weight behind the theory that Victor Grayson was the natural son of one of his own family. Was Campion offered the post as a sweetener, to keep him quiet?

In 1941, Will Hall, Labour MP for Colne Valley, announced that he had discovered what had happened to Grayson. He claimed that he had gone to Australia and died in poverty. When enquiries were made about this claim, the Australian authorities could find no records to support this.

Further evidence of Victor Grayson still being alive came from the

New Zealand Ministry of Defence, when after checking their records they revealed Grayson's medals, the British War Medal and the Victory Medal were collected in London on 25 August 1929. Unfortunately the records of who had actually signed for them had not been retained.

Victor Grayson has never been declared officially dead, nor has anyone proved beyond reasonable doubt that he was alive after the end of 1920, for there are no fully corroborated accounts of him actually being alive after that date. What actually happened to this highly gifted man remains a mystery.

CHAPTER 13

Murder at the *Savoy Hotel*
1923

After marriage all restraint ceased and he developed from a plausible lover into a ferocious brute with the vilest of vile tempers and a filthy perverted taste.

During the evening of Monday 9 July 1923, the orchestra leader in the Savoy Grill at the *Savoy Hotel*, situated in London's famous thoroughfare the Strand, asked the elegantly dressed, petite and pretty French lady in her native language, as she spoke very little English, if she would care to hear any special piece of music. 'Thank you very much', she said in a low voice, 'My husband is going to kill me in twenty-four hours and I am not in the mood for music.' The orchestra leader smiled and said, 'I hope you will still be here tomorrow, madame.' Just a few yards away, sitting at his usual table was Sir Edward Marshall Hall, KC, unaware that this lady would soon become his client.

The lady concerned, described by some as a strikingly beautiful Parisienne brunette, was none other than Marie-Marguerite Fahmy, aged thirty-two, wife of Egyptian Prince Ali Kamel Fahmy Bey, described by one commentator as the wastrel heir to a great industrialist, he had no need to work at anything but pleasure. At twenty-three he had

Front page of the Daily Mirror *Tuesday 11 September 1923.* The Daily Mirror an income of £100,000 a year, a palace on the Nile, two yachts, a racing car and four Rolls Royces. It was widely believed he enjoyed a homosexual relationship with his secretary, Said Enani. Prince Fahmy had fallen violently in love with the former Marguerite Laurent, shortly after she had divorced her previous husband. He pursued her to Deauville and after she agreed to become a Moslem, they married on 26 December 1922.

On Tuesday 10 July 1923 the *Daily Telegraph* reported on one of the worst storms London had experienced in many years, and as the storm raged, it more than adequately served as the effects for the high drama taking place within the *Savoy Hotel:*

The outbreak appeared to travel from the direction of Kingston and Richmond. Soon afterwards the storm reached London itself, and broke with all its fury at a time when, luckily, most of the theatre-goers had been able to reach their homes in safety. The lightening was vivid to a degree. For over two hours the sky was illuminated by brilliant, continuous flashes that gave the buildings an eerie appearance, and at least once what seemed to be a gigantic fireball broke into a million fragments of dazzling fiery sparks. Equally dramatic were the heavy crashes of thunder which grew in a mighty crescendo, *intense and majestic, and then into a* diminuendo *as the storm swept irresistibly over the city. The storm followed a day of almost tropical heat.*

At about two-thirty am, as the storm continued to rage outside, John Beattie, a night-porter, was wheeling a luggage trolley along the corridor at the back of the fourth floor of the *Savoy,* when Prince Fahmy, dressed in mauve silk pyjamas and green velvet backless slippers, came out of one of the doors of his suite, approached him and said:

Look at my face! Look what she has done!

Beattie did as he had been instructed but saw only a slight pink mark on Fahmy's left cheek. Then the other door of the suite was flung open and Madame Fahmy stepped into the corridor, wearing a low-cut evening gown, fashioned out of shimmering white beads. She began to speak loudly to her husband in French and Beattie was obliged to politely ask the couple to return to their suite so as not to disturb other guests. As Beattie continued to push the trolley down the corridor, he heard a whistle, and believing he was being summoned he turned round and saw Fahmy was snapping his fingers at a small dog, which had apparently ventured out of the suite. Beattie continued on his journey, and as he pushed the trolley round the corner towards the front of the hotel, he heard a loud bang, then another and then a third. The porter ran back to the Fahmys' suite and when he reached it, he saw Madame Fahmy throwing down a pistol. Prince Fahmy was laying on the floor, bleeding from the head. Madame Fahmy had fired three bullets into her husband, from a Browning .25 automatic pistol, one of a matching pair (His and Hers) that the couple always kept by their bedsides. A few hours later Prince Fahmy died in Charing Cross Hospital and Madame Fahmy was arrested.

The trial of Madame Fahmy was held in Number One Court in the Old Bailey, before Mr Justice Rigby Swift, it lasted for six days and commenced at ten o'clock on the morning of Monday 10 September 1923. The prosecution was lead by Percival Clarke, eldest son of a more famous father. Madame Fahmy was defended by the formidable Sir Edward Marshall Hall, arguably the most famous defender of all time, who used Madame Fahmy in the witness box to great effect by getting her to reveal her husband's perverted sexual practices. When Marshall Hall questioned Said Enani, Prince Fahmy's secretary, he gained Madame Fahmy the sympathy of the jury:

Sir Edward *Was he in the habit of beating women?*
Said Enani *He would dispute with them, but I have never seen him beat them.*
Sir Edward *You have known of his intimacies with many women?'*
Said Enani *Yes.*
Sir Edward *You said that you tried to dissuade the prince from marrying her?*
Said Enani *Yes.*
Sir Edward *Did you say he was an Oriental; and passionate?*
Said Enani *Yes.*
Sir Edward *You were very much attached to Prince Fahmy?*
Said Enani *Yes.*
Sir Edward *Was he infatuated with her at that time?*
Said Enani *Yes, very much in love with her.*

Enani told the Court that the question of marriage had first been raised in Cairo. Two of the stipulations in the contract were to be that as his wife Madame Fahmy would not be required to wear Egyptian clothes and she would have the right to divorce her husband. Madame Fahmy had agreed to adopt the Moslem religion because Fahmy's mother had left him a large legacy, which was conditional on him marrying a Moslem. However, it seems the Prince was not a man of his word, because when the religious ceremony took place he refused to allow the divorce clause but he retained the right himself, which meant he could divorce his wife without giving her a penny. He was also able to take three wives if he so wished.

Sir Edward *On February 21st was there a very serious scene? Do you know that he swore on the Koran to kill her?*
Said Enani No.
Sir Edward *Do you know that she was in fear of her life?*
Said Enani *No, I never knew that.*
Sir Edward *On the 23rd, did Fahmy take her on his yacht at Luxor?*
Said Enani Yes.
Sir Edward *Were there six black servants on board?*
Said Enani *Yes.*
Sir Edward *I suggest from that moment Fahmy began to treat her with persistent cruelty.*
Said Enani *I cannot say cruelty. He was a bit unkind.*
Sir Edward *The day he arrived at Luxor, did he smack her face, tell her she must not leave the yacht, and then kick her?*
Said Enani *I have not seen him kick her. I knew he locked her in.*

Marshall Hall was able to extract additional information which showed Fahmy in a bad light. Enani said that he remembered an incident when the Prince struck his wife a violent blow and dislocated her jaw.

Sir Edward *When you came over from Egypt, his treatment of his wife was the talk of the ship?*
Said Enani *They were always quarrelling.*
Sir Edward *Do you know that he locked her in her cabin for 24 hours and that the captain had to have her released?*

A cartoon from Cairo's comic weekly Kachkoul *depicting Prince Ali Kamel Fahmy Bey (shown right), his secretary, Said Enani, and his secretary's secretary. It was captioned: The Light, the Shadow of the Light, and the Shadow of the Shadow of the Light.*
Author's collection

Said Enani *I don't know that.*

Sir Edward *Was not the Madame Fahmy of 1923 totally different from the Madame Fahmy of 1922?*

Said Enani *Perhaps.*

Sir Edward *From a quite entertaining and fascinating woman she became miserable and wretched?*

Said Enani *They were always quarrelling.*

Sir Edward *Did she say that you and Fahmy were always against her, and that it was a case of two to one?*

Said Enani *Yes.*

Shortly after the honeymoon, a cruise along the River Nile on Fahmy's largest yacht, Madame Fahmy wrote a statement. This was an exhibit at the trial. Headlined 'THE SECRET DOCUMENT' in newspapers throughout the world, translated into English, the statement ran:

> *I, Marie Marguerite Alibert, of full age, of sound mind and body, formally accuse, in the case of my death, violent or otherwise, Ali Fahmy Bey, of having contributed in my disappearance.*
>
> *Yesterday, 21 January 1923, at three o'clock in the afternoon, he took his Bible or Koran – I do not know how it is called – kissed it, put his hand on it, and swore to avenge himself upon me tomorrow, in eight days, a month, or three months, but I must disappear by his hand. This oath was taken without any reason, neither jealousy, bad conduct, nor a scene on my part.*
>
> *I desire and demand justice for my daughter and for my family.*
>
> *Done at Zamalik, at about eleven o'clock in the morning, 22 January 1923.*
>
> M. MARGUERITE ALIBERT
>
> *P.S. Today he wanted to take my jewellery from me. I refused; hence a fresh scene.*

Marshall Hall suggested that Prince Fahmy was a man of vicious and eccentric sexual appetite. He revealed to the jury that Fahmy's homosexual relationship with his secretary, Said Enani, was a well-known fact in Egyptian society. He produced a cartoon from an Egyptian newspaper depicting Prince Fahmy, his secretary and his secretary's secretary, which bore the caption, 'The Light, the Shadow of the Light and the Shadow of the Shadow of the Light'.

He told the jury:

We know that women are sometimes very much attracted to men younger than themselves, and he went out of his way, with all his Eastern cunning to make himself agreeable and acceptable to her. But this was a man who enjoys the sufferings of women. He was abnormal and a brute. After marriage all restraint ceased and he developed from a plausible lover into a ferocious brute with the vilest of vile tempers and a filthy perverted taste. It makes one shudder to consider the conditions under which this wretched woman lived.

The Prince's proclivity for anal sex with his wife having been raised, suggesting that he used his wife sexually as though she were some unnatural male lover. These unnatural sexual acts caused her to have distressing ailments in an embarrassing place, and it had been Madame Fahmy's hope that during their stay in Europe, she would be able to return to Paris for surgery. However, her husband denied her request, telling her that he preferred the operation to be carried out in London. It was Madame Fahmy's repeated request that she should be allowed to return to Paris in order that her injured fundament could receive the necessary attention that culminated in the tragic events of 10 July. That night Fahmy had called his wife into the bedroom and pointed to a pile of money on the table. She asked him to give her the French money for her to go to Paris for the operation. He told her she could only have it if she would submit to anal sex. She refused and he spat in her face. As she went outside, he followed her into the corridor and took hold of her by the neck. As he tightened his grip she was in fear of her life. Three abrasions on Madame Fahmy's neck, evidently caused by a man's hand were mentioned in the medical report, compiled on Madame Fahmy's admission to Holloway Prison.

Marshall Hall's closing speech was one of his most memorable:

She made one great mistake, possibly the greatest mistake a woman of the West can make. She married an Oriental. I dare say the Egyptian civilization is, and may

The Central Criminal Court Old Bailey. Author's collection

be, one of the oldest and most wonderful civilizations in the world. But if you strip off the external civilization of the Oriental, you get the real Oriental underneath. It is common knowledge that the Oriental's treatment of women does not fit in with the way the Western woman considers she should be treated by her husband ... The curse of this case is the atmosphere which we cannot understand – the Eastern feeling of possession of the woman, the Turk in his harem, this man who was entitled to have four wives if he liked for chattels, which to us Western people with our ideas of women is almost unintelligible, something we cannot deal with.

Marshall Hall's legendary use of theatrical effect in the courtroom was never more so clearly demonstrated than in the closing stages of the trial, when he brandished the gun with which Madame Fahmy had killed her husband, before the jury. He set the scene of the fatal events by crouching in imitation of Prince Ali Fahmy, demonstrating the threat he posed as he advanced towards his wife. Marshall Hall told the court:

... she turned the pistol and put it to his face, and to her horror the thing went off.

The jury was almost spellbound by this demonstration and while he was talking Marshall Hall pointed the gun at the jury, then, to add greater effect, he threw the pistol down on the courtroom floor, the sound of which startled the entire courtroom, and he uttered the words:

Was that deliberate murder? Would she choose the Savoy Hotel for such an act?

Then there came a female voice from the gallery:

No.

And then another:

Of course not!

Marshall Hall then made reference to a work of fiction by Robert Hichens, *Bella Donna:*

You will remember the final scene, where this woman goes out of the gates of the garden into the dark night of the desert. Members of the jury, I want you to open the gates where this Western woman can go out – not into the dark night of the desert but back to her friends, who love her in spite of her weaknesses; back to her friends who will be glad to receive her … You will open the gate and let this Western woman go back into the light of God's great Western Sun.

Marshall Hall pointed to the skylight above where the sun was streaming in and sat down.

Mr Justice Swift concluded his summing up by saying:

A person who honestly believes that his life is in danger is entitled to kill his assailant if that is the only way he honestly and reasonably believes he can protect himself. But he must be in real danger, and it must be the only way out of it.

The jury took less than an hour to acquit. After her acquittal Madame Fahmy said, 'It is terrible to have killed Ali, but I spoke the truth.'

The Savoy Hotel *viewed from Victorian Embankment.* Author's collection

CHAPTER 14

The Charing Cross Trunk Murder
1927

There were several bruises on the woman's forehead, stomach, back and limbs. These, Spilsbury concluded, had been inflicted before she died and he suggested that she had been beaten unconcious and that the cause of death was asphyxia, resulting from pressure on her mouth and nostrils, while she was unconscious.

At a little after 1.50 pm on Friday 6 May 1927, a man described by luggage attendant Mr Glass, as being of military bearing, arrived by taxi-cab, and, aided by a station porter, deposited a large black trunk in the left luggage office at Charing Cross Railway Station. Before he departed, also by taxi-cab, he urged the attendant to take great care when handling his luggage. The trunk was made of wicker-work and had a rounded top, the outside being covered in black American cloth, edged with stitched leather. It was fastened by two fixed leather straps to the front and a wide leather strap, which went right around the girth, fastening with a large buckle, on the top. The letters F and A were painted on either end the trunk and a label read 'F AUSTIN to ST LENARDS [sic]', actually St Leonards-on-Sea and as later discovered, pertaining to the quite innocent previous owner of what was to become in the eyes of the British public of the day, a most infamous trunk. The original owner was in fact Frank Austin, a resident of Hastings but one-time chief high flyer for Barnum and Bailey's circus.

On Monday 9 May, attention was drawn to the otherwise commonplace trunk, when Mr Albert Edward Glass, the cloak room clerk, of 16 Childeric Road, New Cross, noticed an unpleasant smell, which, as far as he could tell, seemed to be emanating from within it. The smell became increasingly offensive and next morning the police were summoned to oversee the opening of the trunk. Divisional Detective Inspector William Steele of Bow Street lifted the lid. He initially saw four brown paper parcels, a ladies' black bag and a pair of shoes. He strapped the trunk up and had it taken to Bow Street

Police Station. When opened and emptied it was discovered that the trunk contained five brown paper parcels tied up with string, a pair of woman's shoes and the aforementioned black handbag. The brown paper parcels contained five portions of a woman. Her limbs had been severed at each shoulder and hip joint and wrapped in items of

The luggage label found on the trunk.
Author's collection

female clothing and a towel, before being wrapped in brown paper and tied up with string. A duster had been wound around the victim's head, which was still attached to the torso. Police surgeon, Dr Thomas Rose, Divisional Surgeon, was called before the remains were moved to the mortuary and properly examined.

On Tuesday 10 May, the *Evening Standard* reported:

> *The body of a woman, with bobbed black hair and blue eyes, and aged between 38 and 40, was today found in a large trunk which had been deposited in Charing Cross (Southern Railway) Station cloakroom. Doctors have found a wound on the body.*

On Wednesday 11 May, at Horseferry Road Mortuary a post-mortem examination on the remains was carried out by Dr Rose and Dr Henry Bright Weir, the pathologist. Home Office Pathologist, Sir Bernard Spilsbury (who had first come to prominence in 1910 in the case of Dr Crippen) also examined the remains. There were several bruises on the woman's forehead, stomach, back and limbs. These,

Horseferry Road Coroner's Court and Mortuary where the post-mortem examination of Minnie Bonati's remains was conducted and where the inquest was held. The author

Spilsbury concluded, had been inflicted before she died and he suggested that she had been beaten unconcious and that the cause of death was asphyxia, resulting from pressure on her mouth and nostrils, while she was unconscious. Congestion in the lungs showed that she had lain on her back for some time. He further concluded that the woman had been dead for perhaps a week, that she had been short and stout and was aged about thirty-five.

Two of the items of clothing bore the laundry mark H51-447 and a name-tag on a pair of slate coloured knickers bore the name 'P Holt'. Through the laundry marks and the name-tag it was quickly ascertained, in fact within twenty-four hours, that their owner Mrs Holt, a genteel lady, who lived in Chelsea, was very much alive. It was she who suggested that the items must have been purloined by someone who had been at some time in her employ, which later proved to be the case. She said the marks were those placed on items of clothing belonging to her servants. Investigations began into the whereabouts of no fewer than ten female servants who had been employed by Mrs Holt during the previous two years, and all but one could be accounted for. Mrs Holt was asked if she would be prepared to view the remains of the murder victim. She agreed to do so, and she identified the dead woman as Mrs Rolls, who had indeed been in her employ briefly, as a cook.

Investigations began and when *Mr* Rolls was found it was quickly established that he was not her husband. She had lived with him for a time and assumed his name but was in fact at the time of their association the estranged wife of an Italian waiter called Bonati. The dead woman's real name was Mrs Minnie Alice Bonati and her maiden name was Budd. She stood five feet tall and was thirty-seven-years-old, and was described by some as a prostitute, who was last seen alive in Sydney Street, Chelsea, during the late afternoon of Thursday 4 May. Minnie Budd had married Bianco Bonati on 27 April 1913 and they had lived for about seven years at 80 Balcombe Street, Dorset Square. At the time of the discovery of his wife's body, Mr Bonati was living at 22 Paradise Street, Marylebone. He told the police that Minnie had left him to go with a roadworker, Frederick Rolls, on 21 September 1923 and they had lived at various London addresses and also at Tilbury, until the relationship came to an end in July 1926. The police were quick to satisfy themselves that neither Mr Rolls nor Mr Bonati were in any way connected with the murder and mutilation of Minnie Alice Bonati.

The Westminster coroner, Mr Ingleby Oddie opened the inquest on Friday 13 May and after evidence had been given by Bianco Bonati,

Detective Inspector Steele and a railway official, the hearing was adjourned for a month until 13 June. The *Evening Standard* reported:

> *Bianco Bonati, the husband, who is an Italian waiter, told how he married the woman in 1913, and in 1923 she left him for their lodger, Frederick Roles [sic], a roadman. He had seen her several times since, he said, and had given her money ... Bonati said he identified his wife by, among other things, her very small ears ...*

The requests for information that appeared in newspaper reports produced some highly satisfactory results. Mr Glass's description of the trunk's depositor was corroborated when a second-hand dealer in luggage named George Henry Ward, from 71 Brixton Road, came forward and recognized the trunk as one he had sold for 12*s* 6*d* to a well-dressed military looking gentleman, of average height, well spoken, dark and with a small moustache. A shoe-shine boy came forward, as he had handed a left-luggage ticket in at the cloak room (placed on one side in case the owner came to redeem it), which he had seen dropped out of the window of a taxi cab in the station forecourt, as the cab drove away, which proved to be the very ticket that related to the trunk, Ticket No. 014190; and the driver of that same taxi cab the shoe-shine boy had seen driving away, came forward with information which was to prove crucial in the rapid detection of the culprit. He told the police that shortly after 1 pm on Friday, 6 May, he had taken two young men from the Royal Automobile Club in Pall Mall, to the police station in Rochester Row, SW1. It was later established from the charge sheet there that the men had been summonsed for motoring offences and had arrived at the station at 1.35 pm. The cabbie said that after he had dropped off the two young men he was hailed by a gentleman who was standing in the doorway of some offices diagonally opposite, which he later identified as 86, Rochester Row, described as rather run-down office suites, situated above the Co-operative stores. At the man's request he assisted him in carrying a heavy trunk

Rochester Row Police Station, seen here in August 2005. The former Police Station is being incorporated in a development of luxury flats. The author

from the doorway of the building and into his cab. Having commented on its weight, the cabbie was informed that the trunk contained books. The trunk being loaded and his fare ensconced in the passenger seat, they set off for Charing Cross Station, whereupon on arrival, the man was assisted in taking the trunk (identified by the cabbie as being the very same one in which Minnie Bonati's remains were found) to the left luggage office by a station porter.

Routine investigations revealed that one of the occupants of a two-roomed, second-floor office that overlooked the street, was one John Robinson, who traded as an estate agent under the business name 'Edwards and Co., Business Transfer Agents'. The investigating officers also established that Mr Robinson had not been seen for several days. Apart from a cracked window pane and a broken fender in the fireplace, nothing seemed amiss, and the police could find no traces of blood.

The funeral of Minnie Alice Bonati took place on Tuesday 17 May 1927. The departure of the open hearse, draped with purple and drawn by two black horses, was accompanied by three funeral coaches. The coffin was of polished oak. The cortege left Mrs Bonati's mother's house in Upper Park Place, Marylebone at 1 pm, watched by several thousand people. Interment took place at Hendon Park Cemetery, Mill Hill. Minnie was buried in a common grave, No.31070 and despite her being the last to be buried in that particular plot (I was reliably informed by the female clerk at the cemetery office, when I visited and was shown the book with the entries for plot No. 31070, that Minnie's coffin was the ninth to be interred in that plot), no memorial was ever erected.

Further investigations by the police revealed that John Robinson employed a clerk, Miss Moore. She was traced and interviewed. She said that on Wednesday 4 May, Mr Robinson had returned to the office at about 3.00 pm in a state of drunkenness, with a man in a military uniform. Alarmed at her employer's behaviour, she left the office early that day, at 3.30 pm and never returned. At the subsequent trial, Miss Moore told the jury she was offered a cigarette and Robinson touched her on the face. She was so frightened that she decided to go home early and not return again. When the police visited Robinson's lodgings in Camberwell Gate, they discovered that the bird had flown, without leaving a forwarding address. However, they had a lucky break when they found that a telegram addressed to 'Robinson, Greyhound Hotel Hammersmith', had been returned to his lodgings marked addressee unknown. As was later discovered, the telegram had been returned to the sender by a new maid at the *Greyhound,* who was unaware that the Robinson mentioned in the telegram actually worked at the hotel. However, this was not John Robinson himself, but *Mrs* Robinson.

Thirty-six-year-old John Robinson was born in Leigh, Lancashire. He left school at the age of twelve and began his working life as an errand-boy for the Co-op. He also worked as a clerk, a tram-conductor, bartender and butcher's assistant. He had four children by his first wife, whom he married in 1911. He later bigamously married a Tasmanian girl from whom he was estranged and at the time the murder was committed, she worked at the *Greyhound Hotel*, Hammersmith. Whether it was the discovery that she had been subjected to a bigamous marriage by her estranged 'husband' that led to her cooperating with the police, cannot be said for certain, but cooperate she did, when after being contacted by Robinson, at his request, she agreed to meet him. On Thursday 19 May, they met at a public house, the *Elephant and Castle*, Walworth. Of course, 'Mrs' Robinson did not go to meet her husband alone. She was escorted by Chief Inspector George Cornish of Scotland Yard.

On being confronted by Chief Inspector Cornish, John Robinson was surprisingly quite amenable, and agreed to being interviewed at Scotland Yard that evening and also to attend an identity parade. At the interview Robinson denied any knowledge of either buying the trunk or of Mrs Bonati. At the identity parade Robinson was fortunate. Of the three witnesses who attended, the station porter, the taxi-driver and Mr Ward, the dealer who had sold the trunk, not one of them recognized him. The police had no alternative but to release him.

A meeting was convened at Scotland Yard on Saturday 21 May at which all the evidence was reviewed. Chief Inspector Cornish decided that the bloodstained, dirty duster, in which the murder victim's head had been wound should be washed to see if it revealed any further clues. Once the congealed blood and grime had been removed from the fabric a small tab on the hem of the duster revealed the name 'GREYHOUND'. A further painstaking search of Robinson's office suite in Rochester Row revealed a bloodstained match, which had been caught in the wicker-work of a waste-paper basket. A small clue, yes, but the bloodstained match, combined with the duster proved sufficient to break Robinson's confidence and having been brought back to Scotland Yard from his lodgings in De Laune Street, Kennington, on Monday 23 May, he decided to make a statement.

Robinson told the police that Minnie Bonati had propositioned him at Victoria railway station at about 4.15 pm on the afternoon of Wednesday 4 May. When they arrived at his office suite, Robinson said that his female companion asked him for money and when he told her he hadn't any, the woman became abusive and threatened violence. There was a struggle in which he broke a window pane as he stumbled backwards and his head hit it. She fell, knocking herself insensible as she struck her head on a chair. Fearful of the racket they had made and well aware of the close proximity of the police station, in a panic, Robinson said he decided to leave the office building. He said he thought the woman was only dazed and would soon recover and go home. However, on his return to the office the following morning, much to his surprise, he found Mrs Bonati was lying face-down on the carpet and she was dead. At no time did Robinson ever admit to killing Minnie Bonati but he did not deny that he had cut up her body and placed the remains in the trunk. At his trial, when asked why he did not go to the police, he replied, 'Because I was in a blue flunk and did not know what to do.' He said that he bought a carving-knife from Staines' Kitchen Equipment Shop in Victoria Street and set about dismembering the body.

Having wrapped the pieces in her own clothes, a towel and the duster, he parcelled up her remains in brown paper, then left the office. The following morning, he returned to the office with the trunk, which he had purchased especially and had transported it by omnibus. The conductor had helped him carry the trunk to the upper deck. He disembarked in Vauxhall Bridge Road at about 10 am, then dragged the trunk along Rochester Row and up the stairs of No. 86 to his office suite. He placed the parcelled up remains of Mrs Bonati inside the trunk, as well as her shoes and her handbag. Having dragged the trunk out onto the landing, he then set about cleaning up the suite of two rooms. He scrubbed, cleaned and polished until he was satisfied that any trace of Mrs Bonati was gone. He almost succeeded. But for the bloodstained match, with only the name 'GREYHOUND' on the duster wrapped around Minnie's head, the

Rochester Row, seen here in August 2005. 86 Rochester Row, the site of Minnie Bonati's murder has now been incorporated in the large office building at 100 Rochester Row, seen here. The author

police would have been hard pressed to have obtained a conviction against him. The cleaning up being done, Robinson retired to a nearby pub at around noon. There he met a Mr Judd with whom he struck up a conversation. As they talked Robinson mentioned he was in business as an estate agent and Mr Judd expressed interest in a flat Robinson mentioned to him, which was to let. Mr Judd returned with Robinson to 86 Rochester Row, where he was given details of the flat. Robinson asked Mr Judd if he would mind helping him carry the trunk on the landing downstairs. Mr Judd obliged and he asked Robinson if he was travelling in lead, as the trunk was so heavy. Robinson replied 'No, I'm taking some books to the country.' It was shortly after this that Robinson hailed the taxi-cab that was to take himself and the trunk to Charing Cross Railway Station. The knife he had used to cut up the body, he buried under a white may tree on Clapham Common, which was later recovered.

On Tuesday 24 May, at Thames Police Court, John Robinson was remanded, charged with the murder of Mrs Minnie Alice Bonati. The *Evening Standard* reported:

> *The premises, 86, Rochester-row, Westminster, where, according to the wording of the charge, the murder was alleged to have taken place, are directly opposite the police court, close to the police station, and only a few yards from the mortuary where the inquest on Mrs Bonati was opened.*

The trial of John Robinson was held at the Old Bailey and began on Monday 11 July 1927. The judge was Mr Justice Rigby Swift, with Mr Percival Clarke leading for the Crown, assisted by Mr Christmas Humphreys. Robinson's defence was ably conducted by Mr Lawrence Vine, assisted by barristers Mr M D Lyon, the Somerset and MCC

Former Thames Police Court, Rochester Row, situated immediately across the street from Robinson's office, seen here in August 2005, where Robinson appeared before magistrates. The former court is being incorporated in a luxury flats development. The author

cricketer and Mr G D Roberts, the former English rugby international. Despite his efforts, Mr Vine was unable to convince the jury that Minnie Bonati was the victim of an unfortunate accident. In his own evidence Robinson admitted virtually everything that was put to him, excepting an intention to kill. The defence called Dr Bronte to dispute the evidence given by the police surgeon and Sir Bernard Spilsbury. Robinson contended that he found Mrs Bonati face down, on the morning of Thursday 5 May. Dr Bronte said that she could have suffocated with her face in the folds of the carpet (which the prosecution showed to have been threadbare), or in the crook of her elbow. He also disputed Sir Bernard's comments regarding the bruising on the victim's body, caused several hours before death took place. He suggested that they could have been inflicted before Robinson met her. However, Spilsbury's contention that the bruises on Mrs Bonati had been caused by direct blows and pressure and that she had been asphyxiated after a violent assault, seemed to hold more water with both the judge and the jury. Another defence witness, the victim's stand-in husband, Mr Frederick Rolls, told the court that Minnie was much addicted to drink and was sometimes very violent. He added that she had attacked him many times. Perhaps it was Robinson's reply to a question put to him by the judge Mr Justice Swift, that finally sealed his fate. When the judge asked why he did not seek help for the unconscious woman lying on his office floor, why, when he realized that she was dead, he did not summon the police to explain matters, Robinson replied, 'I did not see it in that light.'

On Wednesday 13 July, after deliberating for about an hour, the jury returned a verdict of 'Guilty'. Mr Justice Swift donned the customary black cap and pronounced sentence of death on the prisoner. John Robinson was hanged at Pentonville Prison on 12 August 1927 and buried within its precincts.

Hendon Park Cemetery, Mill Hill, the site of Minnie Bonati's grave. She was the last of nine burials in common grave No. 31070, which faces diagonally outwards to the left of the image and is situated directly beneath the bench. The author

Sources & Further Reading

Chapter 1
Foul Deeds and Murder through the Ages, 1236–1984
The Chronicles of Newgate Arthur Griffiths. Bracken Books, London (Originally published
    1883, this edition published 1987)
The Complete Newgate Calendar Vol 111. Collated & Edited by J L Rayner & G T Crook.
    Privately printed for the Navarre Society Limited, London MCMXXVI
The History Today Companion to British History Edited by Juliet Gardiner & Neil Wenborn.
    Colin & Brown Limited, London (1995)
The Illustrated Police News 6 July 1867
Tyburn London's Fatal Tree Alan Brooke & David Brandon. Sutton Publishing, Stroud
    (2004)
Tyburn Tree Its History And Annals Alfred Marks. Brown, Langham & Co., London (1908)
A Man of Singular Virtue A L Rowse. The Folio Society, London (1980)*Notable Historical
    Trials Volume 1* Selected & Edited by Justin Lovill, The Folio Society, London (1999)
English Treason Trials C G L Du Cann. Frederick Muller Limited, London (1964)
The Book of Knowledge Volumes 2 & 3 Edited by Gordon Stowell. The Waverley Book
    Company Ltd, London (1952)
The Oxford Companion to the Theatre Fourth Edition. Phyllis Hartnoll. Oxford University
    Press, Oxford (1995)
Byron Andre Maurois. D Appleton and Company, New York (1930)
Byron Elizabeth Longford. Hutchinson of London in association with Weidenfield and
    Nicholson, London (1976)
Byron Frederick Raphael. Sphere Books Ltd, London (1982)
THE MURDER CLUB TRUE TALES OF DARK DEEDS AND ARCH FIENDS Brian
    Lane. Harrap Books Ltd, London (1988)
Murderers' London Ivan Butler. Robert Hale, London (1992)
Murder Guide To London Martin Fido. Grafton Books (1987)
The New Murderers' Who's Who J H H Gaute and Robin Odell. Harrap Books Ltd, London
    (1989)
The Murders of the Black Museum 1870–1970 Gordon Honeycombe. Bloomsbury Books,
    London (1984)
Murder In High Places Jonathan Goodman. Guild Publishing, London (1986)
Trail Of Havoc Patrick Marnham. Guild Publishing, London (1987)
Real Life Crimes And How They Were Solved Nos. 52, 57, 87 Various authors. Eaglemoss
    Publications Ltd (2004)
Mad Frank's London Frankie Fraser with James Morton. Virgin Books Ltd, London
    (2001)
Evening News 14, 15, 21 March, 28 April, 7 June 1922, 10, 11, February, 27, 28 April,
    25 June 1942, 29, 30 April, 19 September 1947, 18, 19 April 1984.
The Star 10, 11 February, 27, 28 April, 25 June 1942
Evening Standard 14, 15, 16, 21 March, 28 April, 7 June 1922, 10, 11 February, 27, 28
    April, 25 June 1942, 29, 30 April 1947 16, 17, 18 April 1984
The Times 15 March, 28 April 1922, 8 June 29 April, 26 June 1942, 30 April, 20
    September 1947, 16, 17, 18, 19 1984
Daily Mirror 8 June 1922, 26 June 1942, 30 April, 1 May, 20 September 1947
News Chronicle 30 April 1947
Daily Express 30 April, 20 September 1947, 20 January 1975
Daily Mail 8 June 1922, 30 April, 20 May 1947, 18 April 1984

Chapter 2
Gunpowder Treason and Plot 1605
Historical Trials Volume 1 Selected & Edited by Justin Lovill, The Folio Society, London
    (1999)
English Treason Trials C G L Du Cann. Frederick Muller Limited, London (1964)
A History of the English-Speaking Peoples Volume 2 Winston S Churchill. Cassell &
    Company Ltd (1956)
The Tudors & Stuarts M M Reese. Edward Arnold (Publishers) Ltd, London (1940)

England Under the Stuarts G M Trevelyan. Methuen & Co Ltd, London (1904)
Britain And The Stuarts D L Farmer. G Bell and Sons Ltd (1967)
The Stuart Age Barry Coward. Longman, London (1980)

Chapter 3
Execution of Charles 1, Whitehall, 1649
The Moderate 23–30 January 1648 (1649 by our present reckoning of New Year)
The Trial of Charles I C V Wedgewood . Collins, London (1964)
Clough's Stuart Period Ralph Holland & Co., London (1898)
Cavaliers And Roundheads Christopher Hibbert. BCA, London (1993)
Death to the King The English Civil War C L Alderman. Bailey Brothers and Swinfen Ltd.,
    Folkestone (1973)
A History of the English-Speaking Peoples Volume 2 Winston S Churchill. Cassell &
    Company Ltd, London (1956)
Historical Trials Volume II Selected & Edited by Justin Lovill, The Folio Society, London
    (1999)
The Common Hangman James Bland. Ian Henry Publications, Hornchurch (1984)
Lord High Executioner Howard Engel. Firefly Books, Ontario (1996)
House of Commons Journals 8 Feb 1649
King Charls [sic] *His Speech Made Upon the Scaffold at Whitehall-Gate.* Published by
    Special Authority and printed by Peter Cole, Cornhill, London (1649) Guildhall
    Library Pam 4229

Chapter 4
Claude Duval, the Dashing Highwayman 1670
Tyburn Tree Its History And Annals Alfred Marks. Brown, Langham & Co, London (1908)
The Crimson Book of Highwaymen Peter Newark. Jupiter Books, London (1979)
The Chronicles of Newgate Arthur Griffiths. Bracken Books, London (Originally published
    1883, this edition published 1987)
Criminal London Mark Herber. Phillimore & Co. Ltd., London (2002)
The Complete Newgate Calendar Vol 1. Collated & Edited by J L Rayner & G T Crook.
    Privately printed for the Navarre Society Limited, London MCMXXVI

Chapter 5
The Burning of Catherine Hayes 1726
Criminal London Mark Herber. Phillimore & Co. Ltd., Chichester (2002)
Tyburn Tree Its History And Annals Alfred Marks. Brown, Langham & Co, London (1908)
The Chronicles of Newgate Arthur Griffiths. Bracken Books, London (Originally published
    1883, this edition published 1987)
The Common Hangman James Bland. Ian Henry Publications, Hornchurch (1984)
The Complete Newgate Calendar Vol III. Collated & Edited by J L Rayner & G T Crook.
    Privately printed for the Navarre Society Limited, London MCMXXVI
World Famous Crimes of Passion Colin & Damon Wilson. Siena, an imprint of Parragon
    Book Service Ltd, London (1996)
Chapter 6
Murdered by a Poet 1727
The Chronicles of Newgate Arthur Griffiths. Bracken Books, London (Originally published
    1883, this edition published 1987)
Gay Was The Pit Robert Gore-Browne. Max Reinhardt, London (1957)
The Artificial Bastard Clarence Tracy. University of Toronto Press (1953)
An Account of the Life of Mr. Richard Savage Samuel Johnson, London (1744)
The Complete Newgate Calendar Vol III. Collated & Edited by J L Rayner & G T Crook.
    Privately printed for the Navarre Society Limited, London MCMXXVI

Chapter 7
Killed in a Tiff Over a Wig 1735
Authentic Memoirs of the Late Mr. Charles Macklin. Frances Asprey Congreve. Printed for
    J. Barker Dramatic Repositary, Russell Court, Drury Lane (1798)
An Apology for the Conduct of Mr. Charles Macklin, Comedian (1773) Guildhall Library
    Pam 4035
Charles Macklin Edward Abbott Parry. Kegan Paul, Trench, Trubner & Co., Ltd, London
    (1891)

The Chronicles of Newgate Arthur Griffiths. Bracken Books, London (Originally published 1883, this edition published 1987)
The Oxford Companion to the Theatre Fourth Edition. Phyllis Hartnoll. Oxford University Press, Oxford (1995)

Chapter 8
Shot by an Amorous Clergyman 1779
The Insatiable Earl N A M Rodger. Harper Collins Publishers, London (1993)
The Case and Memoirs of Miss Martha Reay Printed for M Folingsby, Temple Bar; and C Fourdrinier, Charing Cross London (1779)
The Case and Memoirs of the Late Rev. James Hackman Printed by G Kearsley, Fleet Street, London (1779)
Literary and Miscellaneous Memoirs J Craddock, London, 4 vols. (1828)
The Chronicles of Newgate Arthur Griffiths. Bracken Books, London (Originally published 1883, this edition published 1987)
Tyburn Tree Its History And Annals Alfred Marks. Brown, Langham & Co, London (1908)
The Complete Newgate Calendar Vol IV. Collated & Edited by J L Rayner & G T Crook. Privately printed for the Navarre Society Limited, London MCMXXVI
The Common Hangman James Bland. Ian Henry Publications, Hornchurch (1984)

Chapter 9
Assassination of the Prime Minister 1812
The Chronicles of Newgate Arthur Griffiths. Bracken Books, London (Originally published 1883, this edition published 1987)
The Complete Newgate Calendar Vol V. Collated & Edited by J L Rayner & G T Crook. Privately printed for the Navarre Society Limited, London MCMXXVI
The Murder Guide Brian Lane. Robinson Publishing, London (1991)
Criminal London Mark Herber. Phillimore & Co. Ltd, Chichester (2002)
The Common Hangman James Bland. Ian Henry Publications, Hornchurch (1984)

Chapter 10
The Cato Street Conspiracy 1820
Lord High Executioner Howard Engel. Firefly Books, Ontario (1996)
Criminal London Mark Herber. Phillimore & Co. Ltd, Chichester (2002)
English Treason Trials C G L Du Cann. Frederick Muller Limited, London (1964)
The Complete Newgate Calendar Vol V. Collated & Edited by J L Rayner & G T Crook. Privately printed for the Navarre Society Limited, London MCMXXVI
The Cato Street Conspiracy John Stanhope. Jonathan Cape Ltd, London (1962)
The Chronicles of Newgate Arthur Griffiths. Bracken Books, London (originally published 1883, this edition published 1987)

Chapter 11
Murder at the Adelphi 1897
The Life of William Terriss, Actor Arthur J Smythe. Archibald Constable, London (1898)
Mr And Mr. Bancroft: On and off the Stage Squire and Marie Bancroft. Bentley, London (1889)
Between Ourselves Seymour Hicks. Cassell and Company Limited, London (1930)
Myself and Others Jessie Millward(in Collaboration with J B Booth). Hutchinson & Co., London (1923)
A Player Under Three Reigns Johnston Forbes-Robertson. Fisher Unwin, London (1925)
Exits & Entrances Eva Moore. Chapman & Hall Ltd, London (1923)
Time Was W Graham Robertson. Hamish Hamilton Ltd., London ((1931)
WILLIAM TERRISS AND RICHARD PRINCE Two Characters in an Adelphi Melodrama George Rowell. The Society For Theatre Research, London (1987)
The Murders of the Black Museum 1870–1970 Gordon Honeycombe. Bloomsbury Books, London (1982)
The Green Room Club Ballard Berkeley (1966), additional chapters by Michael Kilgarriff (1988) transcribed and updated by Geoffrey Howse (1994). The Green Room Club, London.
All On Stage Charles Wyndham And The Alberys Wendy Trewin. Harrap Books Ltd, London (1980)

Dundee Advertiser 18, 20, 22, 27, 30 December 1897
Dundee Courier 18 December 1897
Daily Telegraph 17 December 1897
The Times 17, 21, 22, 23 December 1897, 14 January 1898
The Illustrated London News 25 December 1897
The Illustrated Police News 25 December 1897, 22 January 1898
Era 18 December 1897

Chapter 12
The Strange Disappearance of Victor Grayson 1923
Victor Grayson Labour's Lost Leader David Clark. Quartet Books, London (1985)
The Strange Case of Victor Grayson Reg Groves. Pluto Press Limited, London (1975)
Journey to Understanding Percy Redfern. Allen & Unwin, London (1946)
The Problem of Parliament Victor Grayson M P & G R S Taylor. The New Age Press Ltd.,
    London (1909)
Murder By Perfection Donald McCormick. John Long, London (1970)
Maundy Gregory Purveyor of Honours Tom Cullen. The Quality Book Club, London
    (1975)
The Huddersfield Examiner And West Riding Reporter 6, 13, 20, 27 July 1907, 14 January
    1914
London Gazette 13 January 1914
Kelly's Directory 1920
The Times 19, 20 July 1907
The Daily Mirror 20 July 1907, 3 March 1967
Evening Standard, London, 20 January 1915
Yorkshire Post 10, 12 March 1927
World's Pictorial News 20 March 1927
Sunday Chronicle 23 April 1929
Empire News 6 September 1942

Chapter 13
Murder at the *Savoy Hotel* 1923
Murder In High Places Jonathan Goodman. Guild Publishing, London (1986)
Crimes of Passion Various. Treasure Press, London (1992)
The Daily Mirror 11, 12, 15, 16, 18 September 1923
Daily Telegraph 10, 11 July, 11, 12, 13, 14, 15, 16, 18 September 1923
The Times 11, 11, July 11, 12, 13, 14, 15, 16, 18 September 1923
Evening Standard 10 July, 10, 11, 12, 13, 14, 15, 16, 18 September 1923
Evening News 10 July, 10, 11, 12, 13, 14, 15, 16, 18 September1923
The News of the World 17 September 1923
The Savoy Stanley Jackson. Frederick Muller Limited, London (1964)
World Famous Crimes of Passion Colin & Damon Wilson. Siena an imprint of Parragon
    Book Service Ltd, London (1996)
THE MURDER CLUB TRUE TALES OF DARK DEEDS AND ARCH FIENDS Brian
    Lane. Harrap Books Ltd, London (1988)

Chapter Fourteen
The Charing Cross Trunk Murder 1927
Murder Guide To London Martin Fido. Grafton Books, London (1987)
The Murder Guide Brian Lane. Robinson Publishing, London (1991)
The Murders Of The Black Museum 1870–1970 Gordon Honeycombe. Bloomsbury Books,
    London ((1982)
Crimes of Horror Various. Treasure Press, London (1991)
The Times 12, 13, 14, 16, 19, 25 May 1927, 12, 13, 14 July 1927, 13 August 1927
The Evening Standard, London *10, 11, 12, 13, 14, 16, 17, 18, 19, 23, 24 May 1927, 11, 12,
    13 July 1927 12 August 1927*
The Evening News, London 10, 11, 12, 13, 14, 16, 17, 18, 19, 24 May 1927, 11, 12, 13
    July 1927, 12 August 1927

Index